LEADERSHIP
IN THE
SHADOWS

Written By Kyle Lamb

Edited By MSG Kevin Dorsh And Matthew Bucella

TRAMPLE AND HURDLE PUBLISHING

TRAMPLE AND HURDLE PUBLISHING
Nashville, TN USA
Copyright © 2014 Viking Tactics
All rights reserved

Text layout: Matt Frederick

This book is dedicated to all the righteous warriors who are leading in the shadows.

TABLE OF CONTENTS

Dedication
Table of Contents
Foreword: Matthew Bucella
Foreword: Tom Davin
Introduction

LEADERSHIP IN ACTION 3
1. In the Streets of the "MOG" 5
2. Mogadishu, Somalia 13
3. What is Leadership in the Shadows? 15
4. What is Leadership? 19
5. Past Leaders 21
6. Leadership Traits in ONE WORD 23
7. Types of Leaders 29
8. Leaders or Clock Punchers 33
9. Understanding Military Leadership 37

LEADERSHIP TRAITS 43
10. Looking Down At His Feet 45
11. My Leader 47
12. Moral Fiber 53
13. The Bold Leader 59
14. Standards 63
15. A Leader's Courage 69
16. Be Responsible 73
17. Accountable Leaders 79
18. Be Approachable 83
19. Motivation 89
20. Earning Mentality 95
21. Credibility 99

THE MISSION 107
22. Defining the Mission. 109
23. Political Focus or Mission Focus?. 117
24. Commander's Intent 125
25. Attainable Goals - Adjustable Goals 129
26. Avoiding Bureaucracy 135

FUTURE LEADERS 141
27. Selecting Leaders 143
28. What is Your Promotion Process? 151
29. Training Leaders 157
30. Selecting Subordinates 165
31. Compliance vs. Commitment. 173
32. Counseling 177
33. Discipline. 193

LEADERSHIP TOOLBOX 197
34. Are You Consciously Competent? 199
35. Knowledge Dominance. 209
36. Wish List or Checklists? 215
37. Colonel John Boyd and the OODA loop 225

LEADERS ON THE HOME FRONT . . . 233
38. Family Leaders 235

Acknowledgments
Appendices
Notes & References
About the Author

FOREWORD

Today there is a lot of talk about how to increase an organization's productivity and efficiency. Whether it's the business world, law enforcement, or the armed forces, everyone wants a better way to do things. Far too frequently, technology is the answer: a smaller computer, a faster Internet connection, a smarter phone, a better app, or a more intricate network structure. All of that has its place but those who look only to technology for a solution are missing the true answer: People matter most. Technology has absolutely had a positive impact on everything we do but it is still people who accomplish the mission. An improvement in technology may make your organization more efficient but an improvement in your people will catapult your organization towards success. So, how do you improve your people?

Through the leaders in your organization.

Quality leaders will have more of a positive impact on your organization than anything else you could ever find. Leaders give guidance to the rest of the team on how to accomplish the mission. They give encouragement to others in the wake of success or failure. Leaders set the example for their people in the areas of integrity, professional knowledge, motivation, and commitment. They act as a coach, a mentor, and a teacher. Leaders step into critical situations and make order out of chaos.

Unfortunately, there are organizations without quality leaders. Some of you reading this book have experienced failed leadership in the past. You have witnessed the dismal consequences when "leaders" put themselves ahead of the mission and those in their charge. You have suffered under "leaders" who desire career advancement above all else: their next raise, their next promotion, their next contract renewal. You have watched as "leaders" whose professional knowledge is so small, and their egos so large, they unhesitatingly stumble their way to mission failure. Some of you have worked at organizations which are condemned to wallow in mediocrity because of "leaders" who consistently put loyalty ahead of integrity and value political reliability more than professional competence. And then there are the rest of you who will experience all of this in the future.

When failed leaders cannot or will not fix the problem, it falls on their subordinates to remedy the situation. This is not the ideal circumstance but there is no one else left to ensure the mission succeeds. The subordinates will have to set and maintain the standard when no one above them will. They will have to go beyond their normal set of responsibilities and take on a greater share of the task. The subordinates will have to lead. When called upon, will you be prepared to push past the shortcomings of those in charge and finish the mission? Will you do what others cannot? Can you endure and persevere?

If you were motivated enough, or at least curious enough, to pick up ***Leadership in the Shadows*** and start reading it, then you have a desire to improve the leadership in your organization. You may have also had the misfortune to experience the shattering effects of failed leadership and want to know, above all else, how to prevent that type of tragic situation from ever occurring again. ***Leadership in the Shadows*** will start you down the path to those goals. Kyle Lamb describes some outstanding examples of leadership to which we should aspire and more than a fair share of bad examples from which we may learn even more. The conscientious reader will glean many valuable lessons from

Leadership in the Shadows, which he or she will want to take back to their organization. Outstanding! I have no doubt that is one of Kyle's main objectives in writing this book.

Now go out and do it.

If you really want to change things for the better then you must understand that nodding your head in agreement when Kyle puts forth an example of inspiring leadership and shaking your head in condemnation when he tells a story of unethical selfishness is not enough. You must go into your organization and actually employ the positive traits he vividly describes while guarding against the shortcomings he depicts with equal flair, shortcomings to which we are all vulnerable. Employ them not just for the next few days or couple of weeks while they are still fresh in your mind, but every day. To do so will be a challenge but, as Kyle points out, leadership is inconvenient. Leadership is the more difficult path to take. Leadership is hard. Doing the right thing usually is.

Those who take on the role of leadership must understand the responsibilities they have adopted. When you become a leader, you do not, as some have been heard to say, answer to fewer people. Just the opposite, you answer to more. Those in your charge are not a burden to, at best, be managed or, at worst, be dismissed as a nuisance. Instead, they are the means to your success. More importantly, you are responsible for them and accountable to them. As you can see, assuming a position of leadership is not something to be taken lightly.

For those of you in the military or law enforcement, congratulations on your choice; I've been in one or the other for more than twenty years and I believe there is no higher calling than to deliberately put oneself between the light and the dark. You have already made a life-defining decision to put your country ahead of yourself. Are you ready to compound your obligation by taking on a leadership role in your unit? Can you be responsible for not only your share of the mission but also help your teammates with theirs?

Kyle Lamb speaks of remembering leaders who have influenced our lives and I will engage in an indulgence by telling you about one of mine. Early in my law enforcement career, I had the honor to work for a sergeant whose integrity was beyond reproach, professional knowledge unmatched, and who was never too busy to stop what he was doing and help one of his people when they needed it. Through some misguided sense of duty, he even took on the extra burden of mentoring a young officer who was probably too much of a know-it-all for his own good and did his best to turn him into something resembling a useful policeman. This sergeant influenced the lives of countless officers and, even though he has moved on to a different career, still influences the lives of those with whom he works. I know this because when I meet people from his current organization they always ask me if I knew him when he worked for mine. As soon as I tell them I did, they regale me with countless stories about the positive impact he has on their working environment. None of this ever comes as a surprise to me. They all see what is obvious to everyone who worked with him. Greg Kridos is a great leader.

Kyle Lamb extended to me a privilege when he asked me to write a foreword for this book. A privilege which was matched only by the one he showed when I was allowed to read this book before it was published. I hope you learn as much as I did from Kyle's writings and, just as important, I hope you have as much fun reading it as I did.

Matthew T. Bucella

Sergeant Matthew T. Bucella has been with the Fort Lauderdale Police Department (FLPD) since 1994. He was a lieutenant in the United States Navy and a naval aviator. While at FLPD he has been a Field Training Officer, a member of the Tactical Impact Unit, and firearms instructor. He has a B.A. in Political Science/International Relations from Villanova University and an M.S. in Counterterrorism Studies. Sergeant Bucella lectures on terrorism at a variety of law enforcement, educational, and professional venues throughout South Florida.

LEADERSHIP IN THE SHADOWS

FOREWORD

I've been fortunate to serve 6 years as a Marine Infantry officer, earn an MBA at Harvard Business School and continue my leadership education in the business world for the past 26 years. For the past decade, I've been the Chief Executive Officer of fast growing consumer branded businesses including Panda Restaurant Group (Panda Express) and today, 5.11 Tactical. I'm constantly looking for new insights that will help me become a more effective leader and a better mentor to rising leaders. How can I help each one of my teammates achieve their best potential at work, and maybe even in life? How do we attract great people to sign on to our company's mission and ethos? As the competitive landscape shifts, how can we adapt and respond faster? I believe these are universal questions that leaders face each day.

Why should you read Leadership in the Shadows and share this book with your colleagues?

My personal journey with SGM Kyle Lamb's approach to leadership began almost 3 years ago during a phone call. At that time I had just joined the 5.11 Tactical Board of Directors and our company was collaborating with Kyle's Viking Tactics in product development, with selected products carrying the label "Field Tested by Viking Tactics." On the call I asked Kyle how we could improve a particular jacket in our line. "Sir, that jacket just sucks, I'd never wear it out in the field. It might work for someone who stands out in the rain for 3 to 5 hours, but it doesn't work for me. You really should consider some major changes." The message was, I've come to appreciate, classic Kyle Lamb: respectful, heartfelt and straight to the point without any varnish. Kyle then offered a detailed breakdown of the issues and potential fixes. One major challenge with being a CEO is that most people tend to be so deferential that at times I have to cajole criticism out of them. Not so with Kyle. Somehow he combines hard-edged realism with optimism and a "let's make it happen" attitude.

Just last week I was with one of my product developers as we discussed a new boot 5.11 Tactical will bring to market in several months. Kyle has been testing and helping us refine this product for the past year. At a 30% higher price than any other boot we sell today, we're taking a risk that we can compete with some of the best boots in the broader "outdoor" market space. Similar to the jacket conversation, this project started with a question from Kyle when he asked, "Why can't you guys make a better, higher performance boot?" Fast forward to last week as I quizzed my product developer about some of the final changes to the boot. Most of my inquiries were countered with "Kyle tested that feature and made one last change" and "Kyle signed off on the final prototype." That was all I needed hear. I said "Good to Go." If it passes Kyle Lamb's field-testing, it will perform under pressure.

In my combined 30 plus years of military and business leadership, I've met many very capable leaders but few like SGM Kyle Lamb. While many leaders have proven themselves in one or two domains, Kyle has proven himself across multiple domains of leadership. As you'll read in the pages ahead, Kyle rose through the ranks of the U.S. Army and Special Operations Command (SOCOM) to become one of our nation's most highly trained operatives. He learned leadership lessons, both positive and negative, in the arena of close quarter combat where there is little margin for error and the consequences of failure are truly catastrophic. After "retiring" from the U.S. Army, Kyle and his wife Melynda started Viking Tactics, Inc., a combat tactics instruction and product company that has grown from a garage operation to become a well known global brand in its space. Kyle doesn't discuss Viking Tactics in the book, but as a reader you need to know that he understands the world of "profit and loss" because he is living it every day. Finally, Kyle has distinguished himself as a family leader in raising a daughter and son with Melynda while dealing with the often-uncertain separations that come with a career in the military.

So read this book to gain some new insights that will help you become a more thoughtful, direct, and effective leader. Buckle up your chinstrap and prepare to continue your leadership journey with SGM Kyle Lamb.

All the Best,

Tom Davin
Chief Executive Officer
5.11 Tactical

INTRODUCTION

I have written several other books, instructional books, which taught hard skills which are measured by their performance down range. Either scored targets, hits on steel or, better yet, enemies destroyed.

Leadership in the Shadows isn't the same. This book doesn't have an absolute performance measurement. You may be a bad leader and still enjoy a little success but this is probably due to having some really great people performing in spite of you. You may feel you are a great leader but your subordinates don't use this title when they describe you.

This book has taken years to write. I have started and stopped many times wondering if I was doing the right thing or not. I wanted to finish a project that would help those of you out there who want and strive to become a better leader. I also wanted to make sure I didn't alienate any of the officers and soldiers I worked with for many years, therefore many names have been simply shortened to initials. This is intended to protect those with whom I have served. I want this to be a positive experience. This book is not intended to be a war story. There are plenty of those on the shelves already. This book is intended to be read and re-read with the hope you get at least a morsel of leadership knowledge by reading how I have succeeded or failed in my quest to be a good follower and a great leader. Once you find that first morsel, perhaps you'll return to this book and find another.

I was fortunate enough to be led by a few great leaders when I fought against our enemies. I was also fortunate enough to be exposed to some very poor leaders along the way. Believe it or not, I learned almost as much from those weak leaders as I did from the great leaders.

I was also lucky enough to be elevated into leadership positions throughout my career with U.S. Army Special Operations Forces. During my leadership experiences, I worked with subordinates who pushed me to be a better leader as well as superiors who pushed me in the right direction.

This book is not the be all, end all Leadership book. This book is simply the story of my leadership experiences. It is the story of whom I respect, admire and would follow anywhere on this planet. It is also the story of the Leaders who have failed their Mission and their men and what we must learn from their mistakes so we do not repeat their shortcomings.

As you read **Leadership in the Shadows** please remember, I am not an English major or professional writer, simply a soldier who wanted to pass lessons learned onto you in order to make your mission a success. In most chapters we included a *Lessons Learned* section at the end. Consider this a time to reflect on your past as well as your future, this is your homework. Dig deep and take a good and honest look at yourself. Start asking questions about your own leadership styles and life experiences and those around you.

We have a mission; it is to serve those we are leading. You become more powerful when you are empowering others.

Kyle Lamb

"The person casting the shadow should always value and appreciate their "shadow" if not they are standing in the dark."

-- David Herold, South Africa, 2013

LEADERSHIP IN ACTION

CHAPTER 1
IN THE STREETS OF THE "MOG"

We found ourselves in a fight for our lives on the 3rd of October 1993, in the streets of Mogadishu, Somalia. This story has been told, ad nauseam, by several authors not completely tied to the day's activities. I don't want to rehash what happened that day, but I do want to highlight some key leadership decisions and actions that were made.

This is my view, from a follower's perspective, of those leaders operating in and around the "Battle of the Black Sea."

My Team had infiled into the wrong fast rope area that day, it was confusing to be in a sea of blue tarps and concrete construction with little to no guidance from GPS devices. At this point in history, most navigation in urban environments was done using a map as a reference. Mogadishu is a confusing place, everything looks very similar. I was tense, nervous, maybe scared, the possibility of getting shot at will do that to you. Being a bit nervous has always seemed to prepare me by heightening my senses. I was ready to see what might transpire on this sunny day in the Horn of Africa. Once on the ground, we immediately assaulted what our Team Leader thought was the correct building. After entering, we quickly realized we were about a block off from the correct building. Surprisingly, things were going smoothly, our training always seemed to take over, the more confusion the more you relied on past experiences. SFC Jon H, my team leader, called out a few brief instructions and we departed that building headed in the right direction. As we took up security positions in the street, we ensured that we had 360 degree security. This day's festivities were different than the six previous operations we had conducted in Mogadishu. On this day we were immediately faced with armed Somali gunmen scampering from doorway to doorway, slinging lead in our direction. It seemed almost surreal. Once again, the training took over and we started eliminating targets as they presented themselves. I was excited to finally get a chance to use a skill set that I had honed for years. At one point, we even had a six-legged donkey to deal with. Growing up on a farm in South Dakota, I knew that, other than at the State Fair, you wouldn't see a six-legged donkey so, of course, we engaged the donkey in order to get to the gunman using the animal for concealment.

After getting a fix on the target building, Jon pointed us in the right direction. We quickly moved across the street and started to climb back yard walls to get to the correct courtyard. Once there, we realized we had missed the clearance of the actual objective building and the securing of Aidid's Lieutenants. At this point the mission was a success, we had who we had come to apprehend. As we prepared for exfil, the Troop Sergeant Major instructed our team to secure the perimeter around the convoy as they pulled into position outside of our courtyard. I remember quickly glancing down the road and seeing a burning vehicle, the thought didn't compute until later that this was actually one of ours. I was focused on looking for enemy gunman to shoot so seeing this truck on fire just didn't get me excited. As the convoy rolled to a stop, another Team Leader, Matt Rierson, loaded the detainees as well as his team on the vehicles so they could act as security en route to the airfield. We moved back to the courtyard to await further guidance.

At about the same time, the MH-60 Black Hawk piloted by Warrant Officers Cliff Wolcott and Donovan Briley was shot down. I felt a lump in my throat as I watched the helicopter plummet to earth. I wasn't aware of the occupants at this time but I would soon find out. There wasn't much discussion at this time; we had a plan for such a contingency. This wasn't a plan that had come about arbitrarily. Most element leaders were aware of what would happen in just this case. We had rehearsed it and knew we would move on foot to the crash site. The only limiting factor would be our proximity to the crash site. Since we were less than a mile from the crash site, we knew we could stick to the contingency plan.

Foot movement for this type of contingency was the obvious choice when planning to fight in the streets of this God Forsaken city. It was virtually impossible to maneuver with vehicles, let alone support that movement. Therefore on foot it would be. As I looked to the leaders in our Unit, they were calm and collected as they organized their teams to move toward the crash site. It only helped to calm those of us who were younger and less experienced. I could only imagine what was going through the minds of the young Rangers in our midst. Our element quickly moved towards the crash site. As we turned the corner to head into the hornets' nest, all hell broke loose. We immediately reverted back to our core skills: shoot, move, and communicate. Our team would cover each other's movement as we bounded forward trying to pinpoint the location of the downed helicopter. Looking Earl Filmore in the eye as he told me to bound forward was reassuring. If Earl said it was good to go, it had to be fine. As we neared the crash site, a young Ranger, Corporal James Smith, was shot high in his femoral artery. I was within feet of this man when he was shot, so I immediately did what I had been trained to do; apply direct pressure to the wound to slow the bleeding.

As my teammate, Woody, and a Ranger Lt. named Larry P worked together to drag Jamie from the street, I maintained direct pressure on the wound. This wasn't heroic, this was doing what we had been trained to do. I still felt like we were invincible or at least in control.

Little did Woody and I know that our teammate, Earl Fillmore, had been shot shortly after Woody and I had made our last dash forward. Jon H was now working to save his dying friend. Woody and I would end up being separated throughout the night from the rest of our team. I wanted to be confident, but I was scared, I had always known that Jon H would give us the guidance we needed but the distance of only 30-40 yards seemed like miles. We were all fighting to keep the Somali's from over running Super 61 in which Cliff Wolcott's body was still pinned.

Another Ranger, Lt., Tom D, had made his way to the crash site. He also understood the contingency plan extremely well and quickly worked his way with half of his Ranger Platoon to the crash site. He patiently awaited the arrival of the remaining Rangers from his platoon. He knew their element leader, Staff Sergeant Matt E, also knew the plan. Unbeknownst to Lt. D, Matt E, along with the other half of his platoon, had been exfiled from the battlefield. Not only were they taken away from the battlefield, they would never return again. Little did Lt. D know that this confusion all stemmed from a leader not knowing the contingencies for this operation. The substitute convoy commander had stopped and ordered SSG E and his men to load onto the convoy vehicles. Even when SSG E rejected this order he was told to "Get on the vehicles, now." There comes a time as a soldier when you must follow the orders of those appointed above you, even if they are completely confused as to the contingency planning for this important crisis. SSG E was being told what to do by a Lieutenant Colonel and even though the LTC was wrong, SSG E did as he was told.

As that convoy fought its way to the airfield, SFC Matt Rierson, a Team Leader, had taken control of the situation. Someone needed to step up and take charge after the convoy commander received a very minor wound and took himself completely out of the fight. Matt quickly reacted and took control of the situation as best he could. Not only did he fight through the devastating contact and numerous fatalities that the convoy sustained, but once they arrived at the airfield he was a key leader in putting together a rescue force to fight their way back out to our location. Later that night he would help extract Cliff Wolcott's body from the wreckage of Super 61.

Throughout the night we managed to keep the Somalis at bay. We killed or wounded thousands that night, thanks mostly to the unbelievably brave and talented aviators of the 160th Special Operations Aviation Regiment (SOAR), The Night Stalkers. These pilots flew for 19 hours, continuing to support our positions in anyway possible. I, and all the other men on the ground that day, owe a huge debt of gratitude to these American Aviation Heroes.

We stayed the rest of the night. We all knew why we were there. We were not going to leave a fallen comrade's body in the hands of these savage people. Cliff would not be left behind. I had sensed a desperate feeling come and go, a point where I had said a prayer and asked the good Lord to help me with this situation. Good or bad I would need some help. Jon H continued to move men around his perimeter to maintain security. Matt Rierson fought his way to the crash site and led the extraction team in getting his friend's body pried from the wreckage. Woody and I continued to fight from our location.

Separated from Jon H and the rest of our team, we knew we would eventually link up. Once the rescue convoy departed, we moved into the streets to start our run, the "Mogadishu Mile," to some waiting vehicles manned by elements of the 10th Mountain Division. When Jon H was finally able to lay eyes on the remaining members of his team, he ensured we were all accounted for and quickly pushed us to load into the vehicles.

We made a mad dash for the airfield. When we arrived it was as though a weight came crashing down on us. We had made it. I wanted nothing to do with ever being put into a situation like that again. About that time, Jon was notified that we were missing two of our snipers. Randy Shugart and Gary Gordon had gone into another crash site and paid the ultimate price. At the time, we didn't know their status, so Jon quickly motivated us to fill empty magazines and get ready to head out once more. We were never allowed to go out from the airfield again. We would remain there until returning to the states a few weeks later.

Matt Rierson performed gallantly as a leader and was unwavering as a warrior during this fight. He would be killed a couple of days later during a mortar attack on our aircraft hangar which we used for sleeping quarters. He was a bold and courageous leader who all the men looked up to. He always set the example for others to emulate and follow.

Lt. D fought throughout the night with only half of his combat power. It wasn't until returning to the hangar that he realized what had happened to the rest of his men. The confused leaders above him had jeopardized the plan but Lt. D did not falter, he stayed in control of the situation and dealt with the circumstances. If the situation changes, change the situation.

Jon H dealt with the highs and the lows of this grave situation; he was responsible for the outcome of the situation and never shirked his responsibilities. He maintained his mission focus and never let those around him down when they looked to him for guidance.

Gary Gordon and Randy Shugart made a decision to go into the site of Super 64's crash and attempt to save the crew, who were in desperate need of help. The only crewmember that survived, CW3 Mike D, was later taken hostage and held for a few days before being released. These brave snipers did a great service for that helicopter crew. They went into that crash site on their own volition. They were men of character who did not falter when they saw their fellow warriors in need of help. They fought until the very end, as great Warriors do. Both were later posthumously awarded the Medal of Honor, the highest award that a United States serviceman can ever earn.

Later that day, we stood around a television in our hangar watching the bodies of our fellow American soldiers, our friends, men we had been with the previous day being dragged through the streets of Mogadishu…

You should have a pretty good idea how we felt…

Lessons Learned

- During times of crisis, great leaders will step forward and pull the rest of their organization to success.

    "…Ah, but the one, one is a warrior, and he will bring the others back."
    --Heraclitus

CHAPTER 2
MOGADISHU, SOMALIA
1993

I don't want to call Mogadishu my defining moment, I think it is far from that. Some who were there with me have turned that specific point in history into what and who they are. As I often tell students during our Leadership training, "What have you done for me today?" I believe a leader should continually serve their subordinates. It must be that way. Your subordinates should want to complete the mission with you, but they can do fine without you. Don't get your feelings hurt; remember it should always be about your people, not about you.

During what has become known as the "Black Hawk Down" incident, I was nowhere near the top of the totem pole. I wasn't at the bottom, but it wouldn't be a long fall for me. So my perspective from Mogadishu is that of someone being led, which gives a slightly different perspective. As a subordinate, you get a first hand view of how your leaders lead. I often see superiors who can't see what those being led can see. Those being led often get a truer sense of the leader's abilities, good and bad. So does this perspective matter more to the boss or to those being led? I think it applies to all involved, but once again, I was being led, not the leader.

After Mogadishu many things came to light. There were some unbelievable leadership stories, and some very unexpected leadership failures. As you will probably hear several times in this book, failure can be transformed into a success. This book will hopefully be one of those successes; and it developed because of a combat leadership failure, and great combat leadership successes.

I was asked to deliver a leadership seminar for a federal agency. I declined the request because I felt my strengths were as a shooting and tactics expert, not as a leadership speaker. I was sure I could motivate a group of Soldiers or Marines, but I had some doubt about federal law enforcement agents with whom I thought I had little in common. Then one day a video arrived at my door. It was a leadership seminar presented by a leader from the Battle of Mogadishu. I popped the video in the TV and started to watch. As the video rolled, I grew more and more agitated. I finally stopped the video and grabbed a notebook and pen to take notes as to the unbelievable lies and unwarranted bravado that this individual was displaying during his presentation. Once the video finished, I immediately grabbed the phone and called the agent who had asked me to develop a presentation. I told him I was in. I was angry. I couldn't believe that someone would have the gall to out-and-out lie to his students, who were top-of-the-food-chain law enforcement professionals. At that point the work began. I had never really asked questions of those who were there in the street with me, ever. I needed to find out the truth since the only perspective I could discuss confidently was my very limited view.

I was not a leader in Mogadishu; I was being led. This book is, in part, about passing on the leadership lessons I learned from those great leaders who had led me, some of whom made the ultimate sacrifice.

CHAPTER 3
WHAT IS LEADERSHIP IN THE SHADOWS?

My intent is not to have a sneaky title or a "wunderbar" moment when you touch this book. My intent is to pass Leadership Life Lessons on to those of you who want to push the limits of leadership.

Leadership in the Shadows means many different things to me. First, and foremost, is the fact that most Special Operations' leaders are living and leading in the shadows. Their presence may go unseen by many but it is definitely felt on the battlefield. The stories of their achievements and failures are passed around many campfires. These stories teach lessons, good or bad, which hone the steel of their fellow warrior leaders as well as strengthen the resolve of the men and women they lead.

Another way to look at ***Leadership in the Shadows*** is from the perspective of those being led. Truly great leaders elevate, not themselves, but those who serve them to the highest levels of importance. The great leader does not have to stand up in front of the world to take credit for what he or she has done on the battlefield. The great leader lives in the shadows of his performers and producers. He finds success in mission accomplishment.

Last, there are the leaders with whom I have been blessed by being allowed to stand in their shadow, if even for a moment, as they stand up and take charge of a situation. Leaders who have stepped up to the plate and sacrificed in order to attain mission success; their shadow may only touch a few but it could transform the way we, as warriors, do business.

I have learned from good and bad leaders. I have witnessed successes and failures. It is the *Leader in the Shadows* who stands up and decides what he will do with that success. Will he enjoy the spoils of victory and become stagnant, living on his last great accomplishment? Or will he continue to fight the good fight, knowing full well their next mission could be a failure? If, in fact, he has failed, will he use that failure to transform his next challenge into a success or will he simply fade into the shadows being known as a failure?

Men and women across this country, and around the world, are leading in the shadows every day. If you are a leader who is in the trenches, whether it is in business, serving the public, or as a member of the armed services, this book is for you.

As you and I sit around the campfire and discuss these leadership successes and failures, I hope you will take something away that will help define you as a leader. I want to take you and your team's leadership to the next level, thereby increasing your chance at mission success.

If you want to be famous, this isn't for you. If you want to be successful, it is time to start leading in the shadows.

> *"When you die they put two numbers on your headstone and we all know what they mean…*
>
> *But what really matters is what you did with the dash in between…"*

-- Special Operations Soldier making a toast to our fallen mates in a remote wilderness hunting camp, Wyoming, 2009.

I later realized this was a watered down version of The Dash by Linda Ellis, I think I like the Readers Digest version better.

CHAPTER 4
WHAT IS LEADERSHIP?

What is leadership? Wow, that is a heck of a question, and yes, we have just opened the proverbial "can of worms." We love to sit around and argue about military leaders vs. law enforcement leaders vs. business leaders. One mantra I will always stick with is this:

Leadership is leadership is leadership.

No matter the game you play, whether or not it includes life-and-death situations, leadership is very similar. The repercussions that develop from a poor decision in a business setting may not involve life and death situations as we see in a law enforcement or military leadership setting. However, in business poor leadership decisions can have severe downstream effects, both monetarily and professionally. People's livelihoods are still at stake. I will continue to discuss leadership as though your life depended on it. If you are a businessperson, try to put things in perspective. Will your people lose life, limb, or eyesight if you make a poor decision from your leadership position? More than likely not; but why wouldn't you still want to make the best decision possible for your people, your business, and the overall task at hand?

When I think back to the leaders I have met, no matter the arena, certain qualities come to mind, normally on the positive or negative ends of the spectrum. I have met business leaders who are unbelievably motivating. They can develop a strategy to build a mammoth company. They get in there and get their hands dirty as well. But in the end, when all the shine wears off, you realize they are nothing but manipulative and untrustworthy businessmen. Out for only themselves, they have lost the trust of every single person that has had any long-term relationship with them. Are you truly a leader if the end result of all of your games is the destruction of your team? I would guess not.

Now don't get me wrong, there are professionals who built their business to the apex of success and, in the end, they have not only built a great business but also created a work environment which constantly instills top notch leadership skills throughout the organization. Business is about the bottom line. At least that is what everyone tells me. But in the end, if you as a leader look to your left and right, what will you see? Either "Yes men" that want a piece of the pie or truly trusting followers that want to continue to push you and your business, department, or unit to the successful completion of the team's goals. Leaders and manipulators have a very similar set of skills. The difference between the two lies in their true motivation. Do they put their mission and their men first or do they put themselves and their career first?

Lessons Learned

- At its core, leadership is the same across all endeavors.
- If you are unable to put your mission and your men ahead of your career, stop reading now.

CHAPTER 5
PAST LEADERS

Stop and think for just a moment about all the leaders you have had in your lifetime. Maybe not even your direct leaders, but leaders around you, working parallel to you. Don't just think about those leaders who occupy your same vocation. Think back to your mom and dad, sister or brother, pastor, hockey coach or neighbor. Think about anyone whom you might have considerable contact with who fulfilled a leadership role in your life.

Good or Bad

So were they good or bad leaders? Go with your gut on this decision. If you ponder the thought for too long you might just over think the situation. If they were good, what was the one leadership trait that made them a good leader? If they were bad, what was that specific trait that stands out as the culprit for sending them down the bad leader path?

Being in the spotlight does not make you a leader. Working in the shadows, behind the scenes, does not diminish you as a leader either.

The media has blasted so many people who are out in the lime light, propping them up or pulling them down. While silently, or very quietly, leaders in our country have continued to guide us in the right direction. There are unsung leaders performing everyday within the United States Military, within law enforcement, and in the business world. Without fanfare they do their job because they love to lead, they know the mission and they want to get their people to that goal as a team and accomplish the mission at hand.

Lessons Learned

- When you think of these leaders, what is that defining trait that made them good or bad leaders?
- One word, the leadership trait that stood out, good or bad…

CHAPTER 6
LEADERSHIP TRAITS IN ONE WORD

What is your *WORD*?

Now that you have thought about other leaders, think about yourself. If you were to pick one leadership trait that was the most important to you, what would it be?

This may seem like a crazy question to ask, but see if you don't start thinking about this simple question throughout the day.

When I was forced into developing our *"Leadership in the Shadows"* seminar by a good friend of mine with the Drug Enforcement Administration (DEA), Bill Lutz, he asked this seemingly innocuous question of me. I said, "Bill, that is a stupid question." His reply was, "Then what is it, tough guy? Explain what your word is and how this affects the people you lead and those who you are subordinate to." Not as easy as I thought. I noticed I was dwelling on this question throughout the day.

At one point I found myself sitting on the side of a mountain in West Virginia asking myself. "What was my word and why?" After several weeks to a few months I finally had my word…

During my last deployment to Iraq, I filled the position of Command Sergeant Major for our task force. While filling this position I was required to brief high ranking military and civilian personnel or simply answer their questions as to the who, what, where, when, and why of the hundreds, if not thousands, of combat operations that were conducted over a few month period. These operations might simply be a building search in a remote Iraqi town looking for a wanted terrorist or the operation could consist of working jointly with several government agencies to build the picture using puzzle pieces from not only those around the country of Iraq, but around the world. When briefing US generals, you just never knew what they would ask, especially if they were what we in Special Operations call Regular Army. Regular Army generals would sometimes look at the complex operations that were being conducted -- night operations, helo infiltrations coordinated with a ground assault element -- and ask crazy questions such as "Why aren't these soldiers all in the same uniforms?" They completely overlooked the complexity of the mission that was transpiring with extreme precision to eradicate these known terrorist threats.

After one such excruciating question and answer session that I had endured, I headed outside to catch a breath of fresh air and ran into the overall Task Force Commander, General Stan McChrystal. He said, "Kyle, thanks for answering the generals' questions."

My reply was, "Sir, when do I get to ask my questions? I have a leadership question."

He told me, "I love to discuss leadership. What is the question?"

I said, "Sir, what is the most important leadership trait to you? Only one word." He told me he would get back in touch with me.

The next night, before we conducted our Battle Update Brief (BUB), I looked behind me and saw several military personnel sitting patiently waiting to talk with me. I asked them what they needed and they said General McChrystal wanted them to brief me on their *word*. They all had their word written on a 3 X 5 card. I had several great discussions with Soldiers and Officers that night. It really drove home the point of the greatness of this simple leadership question.

By the way, General McChrystal's word was *character*. When he told me this I said, "Character is someone who pretends to be someone else in a movie." He didn't particularly care for my comment, but nonetheless we had a great discussion. Seeing that a man of his rank took the time to think about this question was inspiring to me as one of his soldiers. It is always good to see your leaders thinking about situations rather than acting without thought. More importantly, trying to improve their leadership skills. I have worked with many high-ranking military personnel and believe me, *character* is key in becoming a great leader. Now if only more leaders would come to this realization.

During a briefing at Quantico, Virginia, one attendee came to me at the end of the briefing and told me he had drawn a picture of his word for me. I was a little taken aback. Why would he draw a picture? Was he trying to go for Honor Graduate? Well, once I looked at the picture I was impressed. At the top of the paper his word was written. "Buoyant." Below "Buoyant" was a picture of waves with buoys on top of the waves as well as in the troughs. He had events written beside each buoy. At the top of one wave it said, "Warrant Mission." At one of the troughs was written, "Write Report for Warrant Mission." Each wave described a high point for leaders and each trough had a mundane or boring task listed. The point he was making was that regardless of the situation, you as a leader must stay on top of the situation. You can't just be a leader when things are going well; you have to be in the driver's seat at all times. You don't get to pick the times you want to lead. You are the leader through thick and thin, through highs and lows. "Buoyant." What a great word.

Credibility

My word is *credibility*. That doesn't mean your word is wrong, or mine is right, this is simply my word. I chose credibility for several reasons. First, the age-old question is this: Are leaders made or born? In America they are most definitely made. Chicken or the egg, what came first? Who cares, just cook mine over medium. A lot of good air is wasted on the discussion of leaders being made or born when it is clearly not possible for a leader to be born. You are not born with credibility. You must earn and build your *credibility* by becoming accountable, listening to your people, and, most importantly, performing on a daily basis. That credibility will be earned through performance and life leadership experiences. Secondly, I want to work for a leader that is credible. The more leadership credibility someone demonstrates, the more his or her subordinates will expect it; and the more fragile that leadership becomes in terms of it being lost in an instant. By constantly demonstrating leadership, you are constantly raising your subordinates' expectations.

What your subordinates want in their leader.

This simple question, "What is the most important leadership trait to you?" can result not only in a great discussion with your people, but it will give you, as their leader, the insight to know what is important to them. You are here to lead people. You are not here to threaten or use your power and position to attain their best performance. Now that you know what is important in their eyes, you might just happen to know what needs to be done to satisfy their needs.

Lessons Learned

- What is the most important leadership trait to you?
- Explain why.

CHAPTER 7
TYPES OF LEADERS

I prefer to classify leaders into different categories. I prefer this method so I can quickly catalog these leaders and understand what they are all about. Most of these classifications are based more on a gut feeling than an academic choice. Academically, leaders may appear to be Great on paper, but when your gut feeling or the real world is involved, they may become Bad, or even worse, Malicious Leaders.

Those who are being led should classify their leaders. By doing so, subordinates will get the real sense of what these leaders are all about. True colors eventually show through when people are in leadership positions. But those same true colors may be hard to read for the leader's superiors. Subordinates, however, will see what these leaders are truly made of.

I break leaders into 5 categories.

> *Great*
> *Good*
> *Bad*
> *Dangerous*
> *Malicious*

This may seem simple, too simple to some of you. However, if you look closely at any leader we discuss, I feel they will fit into one of these categories. Maybe you are lucky and don't have to worry about Bad Leaders in your organization. But then again, maybe you also have your head in the sand. Take an honest look at yourself and those around you. If you truly want to be a better leader or help to elevate your organization to the next level, you must be completely honest with your self-assessment and the classification of those leaders around and above you.

Great Leaders

Great Leaders are those who have the real world experiences to make great decisions. They are leaders who their men look up to. This doesn't mean they are pushovers. This means they have the heart and spine to make the hard decisions despite what others may think. Great Leaders have the foresight to see what may or may not happen depending on their decisions. Great leaders have earned credibility and respect from their mates by being accountable not only for their actions but the actions of those they lead. Great leaders take care of their people. They are not driven by promotion. They are driven by mission accomplishment.

Good Leaders

When I think of Good Leaders, I think of leaders who may just be lacking the life experiences or time in their current leadership positions to become Great Leaders. They want to be Great. They want to learn. They drive themselves to be responsible for their decisions and work to ensure that they take care of their people first, themselves second. They may just lack the necessary training or real world experiences required to be a *Great* Leader. Much like Great Leaders, Good Leaders are constantly working to establish their credibility.

Bad Leaders

Bad Leaders are there and that's about it. They have the position. They really don't care about the outcome of the day's events. They are just happy to be there. Bad Leaders do not want folks to get hurt or killed but they lack the decision-making-process experiences to make the sound decisions that are needed in a fluid situation. Bad Leaders sometimes like to be "one of the guys" in situations where they really need to be their own person. Most Bad Leaders come and go and barely leave a blip on the radar screen. Another way of looking at these bad leaders is as *inconsequential*.

Dangerous Leaders

Dangerous Leaders may be living in a make believe or dream world. Superiors have told them that they are Great Leaders and they, in turn, tout themselves as such. Even though the cold, dark reality is that they are truly *dangerous*. Not only are they dangerous to the mission at hand, but they also may end up getting people killed. All leaders take calculated risks that lives may be lost during their time as a leader, but dangerous leaders will make uneducated (we're not talking about academics here, we are talking about real life education), poorly thought out, life threatening decisions. This type of leader has lost or never had any credibility with his subordinates.

Malicious Leaders

Malicious Leaders are absolutely the worst we can find. They are absolutely in it for themselves. They have no interest in the mission or their people. They simply want to check the box to get promoted to the next position. I have seen these malicious leaders in action and have learned from their selfishness. I learned a lot from them and, more significantly, I learned a lot from their disgruntled subordinates—probably more than I learned from most other leaders I have worked around. Of course, I was learning what I didn't want to do as a leader. Malicious Leaders will stomp on my neck and yours to get where they are going. They will have a total disregard for the welfare of their people and the outcome of the mission or task at hand. They will definitely never be accountable for their actions or the actions of their men.

Take a minute and think about the leaders you have been exposed to throughout your life. In which category do they fall? Picking a category should not be difficult. If it is, maybe we need to simplify this selection process even further. What about simply good and bad leaders?

Lessons Learned

- Think about some of your past leaders and figure out which category they belong in.
- What leadership category do you think you belong in?
- What leadership category do you think your subordinates would put you in?

CHAPTER 8
LEADERS OR CLOCK PUNCHERS

Are you a Leader or just punching the clock?

Most folks in the world who occupy power positions want to be known as leaders when they may actually fall in a different category altogether. All positions are important to overall mission accomplishment and success, and you can lead while filling any position. How do you determine if you are a leader or simply punching the clock, and why does this matter?

If you are a Leader, you are in direct control of the leading of men and women to accomplish a mission. Your job entails the decision-making process to ensure that these individuals come and go safely from the objective area. Your job concerns involve mission accomplishment as well as mission failure.

Clock Punchers may also be concerned with the outcome of the overall mission; however, in general their primary motivation is working their job from 9 to 5.

Regardless of your title or position, if you are managing assets to assist the leaders in accomplishing their tasks or missions, and you are doing this while supervising your team of one or twenty, you are leading as well. If you are punching the clock in a leadership position, this negative and destructive behavior will permeate throughout the organization.

Leadership involves the daily interaction with your subordinates: Helping to guide them in the right direction, working to keep them mission focused, ensuring that all of their mental and physical needs are met, and standing in the way of bureaucracy so it does not affect their jobs.

Even if you are a CEO of a large company you may or may not be a leader. I have witnessed extremely large corporations that have very little leadership. They are successful in spite of themselves. I would place their CEO's more in occupying, but not leading positions. On the other side of that coin is the involved CEO who routinely guides the people in their company in the right direction, ensuring that they understand the mission at hand and how he or she intends to get or keep their company moving in the right direction.

No matter your position or title, you can lead. You must get in there and take ownership of your position and strive to enhance the performance of your company or unit. In the military most of the real leadership on a daily basis is accomplished by the mentorship of one soldier to another, it is also accomplished more formally by those who are fire team leaders, squad leaders, and platoon sergeants. In the police world, a great deal of leading is done at the sergeant level. If a Police officer takes charge they are leading, if they are constantly striving to perfect operations, they are leading. If you are working in the business world, your day-to-day operations should be to lead, to make things more efficient, and help those around you to cut through the bureaucracy to become a more efficient and profitable business. And by the way, as a leader, you need to take care of all of your organization along the way. I never said being a leader was easy.

Lessons Learned

- Leadership requires daily interaction.
- Take ownership of your position in your organization and show your leadership abilities.
- Good leadership will help everyone in your organization to be driven to mission success.

CHAPTER 9
UNDERSTANDING MILITARY LEADERSHIP

As a soldier, it is hard to deal with some in law enforcement and business because they look down their noses at me for being a military leader. These folks quickly show their true colors when they make asinine comments such as:

> *"It's easy to lead in the military. You just kill everyone."*
>
> *"Military leadership won't work here. We can't scream at our people like drill sergeants do."*
>
> *"I could make my organization run as well as the military if I could just discipline my people like they discipline theirs."*
>
> *"Military people are so uneducated they are not good leaders or good followers."*

The list goes on. Those who say things like this have one thing in common. None of them were ever in the military.

This can be nerve racking. We actually had a leader at the DEA who said he didn't want to learn from military guys because all of their stories were about missions which went poorly. What this fella doesn't realize is we talk about those missions so others don't repeat the mistakes we made. We have been able to analyze our perceived failures or shortcomings during these adverse mission conditions and wanted to pass the lessons learned to ensure that Federal and State law enforcement personnel don't repeat our shortcomings.

Military leaders are really not much different than the rest of the world's leaders. They do have to be more concerned about what might happen if they fail since death is always a possibility when you are in a combat leadership role. They also have to be fiscally responsible with their budget. When the money runs out, they are out of luck. In the past few years it has been even harder since the government has failed to pass a single budget. When this happens, military leaders don't get to sit idly by until the next year. They have to keep leading. They have to continue to accomplish their mission. No money, no excuses. A lack of funding is not an excuse for a poorly executed mission.

Top military leaders are also held to a much higher standard of conduct than the people in positions of authority over them. Specifically, some members of Congress and the Executive Branch can have severe criminal problems, engage in extramarital affairs, cheat on their taxes, and have massive substance abuse issues without ever suffering any consequences. If military officers committed any of those infractions, they would not only feel the wrath of the civilian courts, but the military courts martial as well. If they cheat on their taxes, they will be relieved of command. If they drink, they will offend the local religious zealots in the Middle East. One high level commander had an affair with his biographer and he was forced to retire. On the civilian side of the coin, there are many obvious and well-documented examples of improprieties by our politicians who do not fall under the double jeopardy of the military system.

CHAPTER 9 UNDERSTANDING MILITARY LEADERSHIP

Military leadership is a tough thing to describe for those who haven't been there. When I deal with Outdoor Industry leaders who have military experience, I immediately get a good feeling. Sometimes they will let you down but most times there is a positive outcome. Military leaders may have difficulties understanding the money side of business, because they never ran a for-profit organization, but the discipline and people skills are generally there.

When I was asked to present **Leadership in the Shadows** to the United States Military Academy at West Point, I was honored. After meeting hundreds of these fine young cadets, I realized they are, at this early point in their careers, still very much preparing to meet the rigors of being a military leader. They do not yet have the training, education, knowledge, or experience necessary to be responsible for successful mission outcomes, let alone the actual lives of those they will be leading. I don't want this to be taken in a negative manner. At this point in their careers they simply don't have all of the answers. But… they are Warriors. They have the Warrior Spirit. They want to do what is right when the time comes to lead the men and women of the United States military. This spirit will carry them through and make most of them successful military leaders. There is a support structure of seasoned Officers and Non-Commissioned Officers (the Sergeants) who will take these young cadets under their wings when they pin on their 2nd Lieutenant rank and ensure they are mentored into becoming military leaders.

Military leaders should be warriors. Business leaders often refer to the "warrior spirit" when discussing leadership. If you truly want to be a *warrior-like leader,* there are a few things you will need to GUARD AGAINST:

1. **Political Correctness.** Political correctness is the first. You must say what you mean and mean what you say. This is critically important. You can't have those who look up to you confused as to what you mean. If you speak openly, you will likely offend those who don't have the warrior spirit.

2. **Racism.** Unlike America, the military has set aside racism. Men and women from all walks of life are treated as equals in the military. In the military, performance is what counts, not the color of your skin. Civilians talk about equality but when it comes right down to it there are different sets of standards for different races. In the military, promotions are based on performance, not on race. Being able to pick the right man or woman for the job, regardless of race, is extremely important to military leaders. Generally speaking, warriors are warriors. We are not Lebanese-American Warriors, not Swedish-American Warriors, we are American Warriors.

3. **Turning off Leadership when you leave your job at the end of the day.** You are always a leader in the military. If someone screws up after hours, you are there to take care of them or punish them. In civilian life, this is not the case.

4. **Distancing yourself from those you lead.** Camaraderie is extremely important in the military. You will be living and working with these people for extended periods of time.

CHAPTER 9 UNDERSTANDING MILITARY LEADERSHIP

5. **A Caste System.** There isn't a caste system in the United States military. Your background and upbringing is never brought into the equation. You are all Soldiers, Sailors, Airmen, or Marines. There are no special esquire titles.

6. **Thinking formal education is the most important item on a resume.** In the military, formal education isn't as important as experience. This principle has been lost in American society. Some think you must have a college degree to be job worthy. This is not the case in the military. This doesn't make military people stupid. It means they focus on experience in order to accomplish their mission not the act of getting a degree.

7. **Believing everyone is different.** Military people have very similar outlooks on politics and life in general. This is refreshing for me. I often find solace being with military people because they are real and I know they will understand my attitude. When I'm with them it is never about the latest, greatest fashion or "being green." It is about the mission. I have a common bond with all military people, active or retired.

Adding to the stress of being a military leader is the absence of family. Long deployments without the support of a family can be very difficult. This may not seem like a big deal until you have been deployed overseas. You don't get to walk away from the stress of the job. You don't get to stop by the local golf course for a round of golf or enjoy a cold adult beverage at night. You are 100 percent in the game from the time the wheels leave American soil until you finish your deployment.

You won't be allowed to see your kid's ball game or attend a school play. This is stress. The more you get involved as a leader the more real it gets. You will become so close to those you lead, the line separating your military family from your home family will become blurred. This isn't easy. It becomes even harder when one of your military family members is injured or killed.

You do not need military experience to be a *GREAT* leader. It isn't a must, but we can all learn from each other. Just as military leaders reach out to learn from business leaders, business leaders should reach out to the military to find innovative or, in some cases, old, combat-tested, and proven ways to lead.

Lessons Learned

- Military Leaders are held to a stricter standard than Political or Business Leaders.
- You don't have to be a former military person to be a Great Leader.
- How can you become a warrior-like leader?

LEADERSHIP TRAITS

CHAPTER 10
LOOKING DOWN AT HIS FEET

Looking down at his feet, he didn't just see a fallen soldier, or a fallen teammate. He was looking at his best friend. He had trained with this young man for many years. They had shared a lot of great times but also helped each other to get through the rough times. They had trained an Assault Team to the highest levels of proficiency in Combat Marksmanship, Close Quarters Battle, and physical fitness. They had planned and rehearsed this mission over and over. They had checked all of their team's gear and mentored young soldiers on the team so they would all be able to get the job done. They were ready. How could this happen? How could Earl be dead? How could they fly to the Horn of Africa to help a suffering country wrought with famine and disease and be treated like this? Mogadishu, Somalia was not where SFC Earl Fillmore should die. He should grow old on his porch with a grand kid on his knee...

Through all of this, SFC Jon H was still expected to lead. He couldn't shut down and feel sorry for himself. The rest of the assault force did not know Earl had died until the Ground Force Commander made a radio call asking the status of SFC H's element. SFC H called the Commander telling him how many wounded he had at his position and that he had one KIA. A while later, the Commander called again asking for the call sign of the KIA. SFC H reluctantly said, "Alpha

Two." This took the wind out of the sails of every assault force member who was monitoring the assault frequency. How could this be? We were supposed to be unstoppable.

Shortly after that call, unsolicited, Jon came back on the radio.

"All elements, this is Alpha One, and this is what we are going to do."

He shouldn't have been back on the radio. That was not how the element was structured. We are a military organization. Other leaders should have been on the radio, yet Jon made that call. His simple call, letting everyone know that he was back in the fight and ready to set aside his grief until the fight was over, was exactly what was needed to get us all back in the fight…

Why did he do this? He says he doesn't know…

But I do. He did this because he is a Great Leader…

Sergeant First Class Jon H is a *GREAT LEADER*.

CHAPTER 11
MY LEADER

My leader was SFC Jon H. Jon was a soldier's soldier and as some would say, "Harder than reinforced woodpecker lips." Now that is hard. He is a great leader, a credible leader, and he was forced to deal with some unbelievably difficult situations in Mogadishu.

SFC H or "Lumpy" as was his call sign. Unlike the Air Force and Navy, Marines and Soldiers don't get cool call signs. Most are degrading or humorous, so "Lumpy" it was.

"Do what needs to be done."

Jon had accepted me onto his team with open arms. He immediately made me part of the team and pushed me to take responsibility. He told me I needed to "do what needs to be done." Get out there and figure out what can be done to become better, whether it be through training, tactics, or technology. If the trash needs to be dumped, get on it. Your rank and position do not make you immune from work. No task is unimportant.

This attitude set the stage for what kind of man I would be working for over the next few years. Jon was absolutely focused on the mission at hand: Hunting down terrorists, no matter where they decided to lay their heads at night.

Accountability

We had a new guy come to our team straight out of a high level Close Quarter Battle (CQB) training course. This course lasts for months and is touted as preparing you for absolutely anything once you get to your team. So when Johnny Cool Guy shows up to the team he is ready for action, there isn't anything he can't handle in a CQB environment. Well it didn't take long for him to get his chance to show the rest of the team his mad skills. The team was to clear a building using their paint marking weapons. These weapons are the same as our normal carbines and pistols with the exception that they fire a paint marking round. They are nothing to laugh at; they will definitely penetrate any exposed skin and give you crocodile tears if they hit the right spot. Most assaulters have paint scars somewhere on their body to show a point in their training that they actually learned something. Unlike most law enforcement organizations, we were not allowed to put on additional clothing except for the covering of the family jewels. If you wanted to learn, it had to hurt. Using these training weapons also allows us to use live role players to simulate enemies and non-combatants, much better than shooting paper targets day in and day out.

Things started out that day pretty simple. Most of the building was cleared without a hitch; a few bad guys were shot along the way. When Jon H's team finally enters the last room in their area of responsibility, they quickly realize there is an adjoining door. Could be a closet or another room, no one knows. The Assistant Team Leader, Earl Filmore, steps around the stack to pull the door open for the team. Wouldn't you know it? New Guy, or Johnny Cool Guy as I recently called him, is the number one man. He is ready. With all the confidence or cockiness in the world, he gives Earl a nod indicating that he is ready. Earl jerks open the door, and there in the closet with his hands up is the hostage. Not only is it the hostage, this hostage is being played by the Troop Sergeant Major (SGM). Well, Johnny Cool Guy doesn't miss a beat. He starts to jump back from the startling situation and quickly shoots the hostage three times in the back of the thigh. His training told him differently but his lack of experience and repetition had failed him. Not a good place to shoot someone, especially when it is the Troop SGM who, as I said, is playing the part of the hostage we are there to rescue. More than a few cuss words flowed in a short amount of time.

The wind quickly went out of the new guy's sails. In our unit, if you have a recurring problem with shooting the wrong person, aka *the non-combatant*, you will be fired. No fanfare or gnashing of teeth, you just leave the unit.

Shortly after the assault, SFC H found himself in the Troop SGM's office. He was being told that the new guy was out. He had a target discrimination problem and needed to go. Jon H wouldn't hear it. He boldly explained to the SGM that it wasn't the new guy's fault; it was his fault. SFC H said *he* needed to be accountable for the new guy's actions; he didn't train the new guy to a satisfactory level before taking him into a complex building-clearing scenario. If the SGM would let him keep this man on the team, SFC H assured him, there would be no more issues after a block of retraining. The SGM reluctantly approved.

So SFC H took the new guy, whose name to this point has been changed to protect the guilty, down range to retrain him on target discrimination for many hours over many days. Over the next 15 years that new guy never made the same mistake again.

I was that new guy. I was extremely lucky I had a great leader like SFC H. The bottom line is this: If SFC H had not been accountable as a leader I wouldn't be where I am today. He would have let me flounder and get fired which would have meant moving back into the regular Special Forces community. I owe him as my leader. If you were to ask him, he would simply say he was doing his job. SFC H is a great leader.

Motivation

SFC H was continually motivating our team. He didn't accomplish this with threats, power, and position. He did this by pushing us all to make ourselves part of the solution to the problem. He allowed us to have "outside the box" type ideas to solve issues.

He also pushed us through competitions, but they were not always physical; it could be a shooting event or a thinking exercise. Whatever the task, he wanted us to push each other, build confidence, and fix problems that we faced. He might not always be there to babysit the new guys. They may need to act on their own. He didn't teach us "what to think" he taught us "how to think."

Bold

SFC H was a bold leader. He was willing to take a chance, try something new. He would stand up for his people. You absolutely always knew that Jon would be there for you in a bad situation. This cannot always be said about some of our leaders.

Moral Fiber

SFC H had moral fiber that was second to none. He was a great husband, great father and a great leader who was trusted by all the soldiers with whom he came into contact. We always knew that Jon was looking out for our best interests, not his own. This is not always common in the military. Serving with a credible leader who is willing to be accountable for his or her actions is not simply a given. Maintaining total mission focus is even harder to find. If you or your leaders are easily sidetracked by bureaucracy, then you are causing your subordinates problems. You should be continually looking at better ways to increase efficiency. The complex objectives or targets that we are asking folks to deal with these days requires us, as leaders, to be extremely efficient. This is impossible in a bureaucratic environment.

SFC H was *My Leader*. He had it figured out. He was able to effectively lead men into battle. They followed him because he was credible. They followed him because they respected him. They followed him because they knew he was technically and tactically proficient. He had been trained to lead and they were all ready to follow; he would not let them down, no matter the circumstances. Now if I could only find a way to emulate him throughout my career.

Lessons Learned

- Do what needs to be done.
- As a leader you are accountable for your team's failures.
- Motivate through shared responsibilities.
- Be a bold leader.

CHAPTER 12
MORAL FIBER

What do you do when no one is watching? How do you act in your presence and your presence alone?

Many look around at military personnel and find it hard to believe that a group of such ugly characters could be great leaders. How could men and women with no college education, tattoos, big muscles, weapon-handling skills, and attitudes be great leaders? In this day and age of political correctness it is nice to see that low level leaders are still making a big impact regardless of how they look. These men and women are warriors who know the impact of leadership, or the lack thereof, on their mission and their people's welfare.

When there are less than morally correct leaders at higher levels it will have detrimental effects on those at lower levels. We see this time and again. When you have leaders who are not morally and ethically sound, they will have issues with the good people they lead. The performers are sometimes punished for their ethics, ridiculed, or singled out for standing up for what is right. Other times morally defunct leaders will take the credit when they shouldn't or shirk the blame when it belongs squarely on their shoulders. They will lie and cheat to make themselves look good or their competition look bad.

In order to gain entry into most Special Operations units, you have to obtain a security clearance which requires a very thorough background check. Currently, many politicians would never be able to pass this test. This is troublesome to those who are laying it on the line every day on the battlefield. These Special Operations men and women know their highest elected leaders are not cut from the same cloth as themselves and cannot stand up to the scrutiny the operators must undergo to simply have the jobs they have.

So what does all of this have to do with *Moral Fiber?*

Simply acting like a good guy in public is not *moral fiber*. *Moral fiber* is a part of your DNA; it is something that makes you tick. It isn't the way you look or the way you talk or the color of your skin. It is what is in your soul. Are you willing, as a leader, to stand up for what is just and right no matter the downstream effects? Are you willing to stand up to another leader who is morally and ethically wrong in their convictions? If you won't, or can't, because you are frightened of what will happen to your paycheck or title then you are not a person with good *moral fiber*. Speaking your mind should not be considered bad in today's world. Now, when I say speak your mind, I am not talking about blowing a gasket and cussing out your boss. What I am talking about is formulating your ideas and speaking up intelligently in order to advocate your position. In today's society it is acceptable to stand up and speak your mind as long as you are from the fringe of society. However, speaking your mind is frowned upon if you are a mainstream, God-fearing, contributing member of society. This must stop. As a leader you must ensure those performers with whom you work are able to stand up and be heard. Those folks with *moral fiber* are the ones who will continue the fight in the right direction.

> *General Stanley McChrystal had been my leader while serving in Iraq. He was always respected for his actions during the good and the bad times of our fight. He had sacrificed for years by being separated from his*

CHAPTER 12 MORAL FIBER

wife and son many more months than any of us had endured. General McChrystal had been successful as a Ranger leader as well as a conventional Army leader. His success didn't dim when he took over the Joint Special Operations Command (JSOC). As the JSOC Commander he was responsible for the highest levels of Special Operations being conducted in Iraq and Afghanistan. He continually delegated by letting his subordinates run the show but ultimately we all knew that General McChrystal was responsible. We had extreme confidence in this man and his abilities as a military leader but, at the same time, he mentored others and helped them become great leaders. His confidence was not cockiness. His confidence was the mark of a man who knew what he was doing. He didn't belittle or denigrate those who were not up to his standards. Instead, he pushed them to attain the highest levels of performance which they were capable of. General McChrystal was beyond reproach with regard to morals and ethics so it came as quite a surprise to all of us when Rolling Stone magazine released an article entitled "The Runaway General." The surprise continued when General McChrystal voluntarily resigned from the Army. Comments in the article led the reader to believe that he or his staff had made disparaging remarks about the President. General McChrystal did not grovel. He stood as a proud leader and quietly stepped down. He had a short meeting with the President who accepted his resignation.

In April 2011, the Department of Defense's Office of the Inspector General released a summary of their review. They found that none of the allegations against him or his staff could be substantiated.[1] The

media did not bring this to the national spotlight and neither did the general. He stood by quietly as he was proven to be the great leader we all knew he was and had always been. General McChrystal knew nothing good would have come from him fighting the allegations. He stepped down and took away the power of the opposition.

General McChrystal's moral fiber is as it should be, hidden until history reveals it. He was an absolute advocate for truth, honesty, and the greater good. He didn't fight for the spotlight. He was constantly leading in the shadows.

Integrity is another word for *moral fiber*. For a leader, loyalty is critically important; both for a leader to show his men and his men to show their leader. But what comes first, integrity or loyalty? U.S. Air Force Colonel John Boyd, creator of the OODA Loop, would often speak to his men about this very topic. He would say, "If your boss demands loyalty, give him integrity. But if he demands integrity, then give him loyalty."[2] Which is most important to you? (Please see Chapter 37: Colonel John Boyd and the OODA Loop for more on John Boyd.)

I can't tell you what to do. You as a leader must look yourself in the mirror and decide what is right and wrong. Choose wisely because this will have downstream effects in regard to your credibility with your people. They know what is going on. You may choose not to give them the credit, but they know nonetheless, so stand up and be accountable.

And perhaps most important of all, be honest with yourself. If you can't even do that, you'll never have any *moral fiber* for anyone else.

Moral fiber is the foundation upon which *Good* and *Great Leadership* is built. Without it, no one can ever hope to be a leader regardless to what rank they are promoted or the position they attain.

Lessons Learned

- Moral fiber guides your actions at all times, not just when others are watching.
- What is most important to you, loyalty or integrity?

"In the end, leadership is a choice. Rank, authority, and even responsibility can be inherited or assigned, whether or not an individual desires or deserves them. Even the mantle of leadership occasionally falls to people who haven't sought it. But actually leading is different. A leader decides to accept responsibility for others in a way that assumes stewardship of their hopes, their dreams, and sometimes their very lives. It can be a crushing burden, but I found it an indescribable honor."

General Stanley McChrystal
US Army, Retired
My Share of the Task

CHAPTER 13
THE BOLD LEADER

When I think about those leaders I call bold, I notice they all possess a common trait. The bold leader is the one who fearlessly gets out in front of his men and leads his team, squad, or platoon to safety or victory.

In Somalia we had a bold leader in our midst, Matt Rierson. On the 3rd of October, Matt rode all the way back to the airfield with the convoy while it went through an unbelievable amount of enemy fire. When the convoy needed leadership, Matt stepped up to the task. He dismounted and got everyone headed in the right direction. While under fire, he ran from vehicle to vehicle getting the men organized and moving. Later that same day, he helped organize the rescue force to come back out into the streets of Mogadishu to save his mates. He did this because he knew we needed help. He knew that his friend, Cliff Wolcott, was pinned in the wreckage of his downed helicopter. Once this rescue force arrived at the first crash site, Matt took charge of the recovery operation. He showed total disregard for his own safety as he jumped through a window to land in the alley which contained Cliff's crushed aircraft. Matt was a bold leader. He performed heroically that day. After the fight, Matt was one of the most vocal team leaders calling for an analysis of what happened in order to

determine what we needed to improve if we were sent into the streets again. Matt Rierson was killed two days later on October 6th, 1993 during a mortar attack on our hangar.

Matt is a real life example of a bold leader. His tenacious attitude pushed his team, and the rest of his unit, to think outside of the box and solve problems. Additionally, he pushed those around him to compete at the highest levels with firearms. He was the best shooter in our unit. He was the man that got me interested in shooting sports and helped raise my level of expertise with the 1911 Pistol.

If you stand up to the enemy, if you charge the machine gun nest to save the day, you are bold and courageous. But sometimes there is more to being bold than just being brave.

I have seen many leaders talk the talk but when it comes time for them to stand up for their men against the bureaucrats trying to stifle initiative, they simply keep their mouths shut and fall in line with the stupidity. No questions asked. We need bold leaders to stand up and fight for their people. This is what I call normal bold behavior. Being bold is often not normal behavior. It takes a confident leader to be bold under these circumstances; one who doesn't second-guess their own decisions. If the bold leader doesn't stand up, the bureaucrats will run over their people destroying any chance of mission accomplishment.

What if?

When I ask leadership students to describe what being bold is all about, many times they say "It is having the courage and fortitude to stand up to the man…"

But what if the man is right? Standing up for a group of your peers is often easier than taking the unpopular position by standing up in opposition to those same peers. If your superiors have made the correct decision, you must do the same thing and stand with them.

This is a problem leaders frequently encounter. You hang out with your peers each and every day. You know their families and you've become very comfortable in their presence. But now it is time to step up and make a hard call that goes against your peers. Remember, this isn't a popularity contest. This is leadership.

Lessons Learned

- Great leaders are not fearless; they deal with that fear and continue to lead.
- Stand up for your people.
- Stand up for your leaders if they are right.

CHAPTER 14
STANDARDS

Everyone should agree we need standards in whatever occupation with which we happen to be involved. There must be a degree of proficiency maintained in order to be productive or effective under certain circumstances. As leaders, you must also adhere to those standards of productivity and conduct. At least I hope that is a true statement.

What if I said:

"You must live by the same standards as your men."

This should not be an offensive statement. It should also not cause you to squirm in your seat. If you are not living by the same standards as your men and women, there is an issue.

In Washington, D.C. we have a group of elected officials who were put there by us, the voting citizens of America. It is our job to pick the best men and women to hold these decision-making positions in the Senate or Congress. There are many great men and women serving but those we hear about the most are the not so great.

As Americans, we should hold our elected and appointed officials to the highest standards of moral, ethical, professional, and responsible behavior. They are the leaders of our local and state governments in the best country in the world. However, many of these elected officials are not living in the real world in the same way you and I do. They are given health care which is vastly different from that which the citizens are forced to use. They are allowed to perform their jobs in spite of criminal backgrounds, which would cause most military and law enforcement professionals to immediately lose their jobs. Background checks are routine for military and law enforcement professionals, the failure of which equates to no-job. Are you aware there are those in these esteemed offices of our great country that could not pass the standard criminal background checks performed on military and law enforcement professionals? Does this upset you? Of course it does! There is no way a normal American can see the one-sidedness of this madness and not have the hair on the back of their neck standing stiffly upright.

In the end, you have to remember we, as the voters in our society, put them there. Ultimately, it is our standards as citizens which have been lowered. It is obvious that one good politician cannot make all the difference by himself. What we need is for all of our politicians to get back to the original standards which were set for them. They are sent to the halls of government to represent the people. Instead, they have raised the level of partisan rhetoric to an all-time high. This was not our intent when we set the standards for their service. So why would you, as a business or military leader, want to have different standards than your people? We all like to get special treatment but, as a leader, why would you want to have special treatment? As a leader, you must be careful to avoid the controversy which you will incite when receiving even small special allowances.

I once had a military officer give me his upgraded First Class airplane ticket simply because he did not want the perception he was getting a special favor due to his rank. He was a quiet professional who was well respected by all who had him as a commander.

> Before becoming a Ranger Leader, you must successfully complete the Ranger Orientation Program (ROP). If you do not pass this course, you are forced to leave the Regiment and go wherever the Army may need you. One individual from our Mogadishu days didn't pass ROP yet, through political ties, was still able to continue to his leadership position within the Regiment. This failure was known by many around him. How do you think this made his young Rangers feel? They were crushed. If a lieutenant failed ROP, he would be gone. Yet this senior leader did not pass and, due to his connections with high-ranking officers, was allowed to skate through. It was eventually proven during the Battle that he was lacking many traits which are needed to be a combat commander. This was not only his failure, by not declining a position he was incapable of, it was the failure of the regimental commander at the time who allowed this promotion to occur. Failures generally lead back to a bad leader. The Rangers who created ROP knew why they did it, for just this purpose; to weed out the weak from the performers. The system had worked right up until the "good ol' boy network" threw a monkey wrench into it.

If you are a law enforcement professional who must maintain a certain level of physical fitness and weapon proficiency throughout the year, then you must continue to maintain these standards even when you move into a leadership position. You don't need to be the fastest runner or the best shooter, but you must maintain the standards which you ask your people to maintain.

It is a simple matter to let those around you see what you are really made of. If you don't perform, how can you ask them to? If you can show your people that you are trying to maintain some semblance of standards, they will be right there with you. If you look down your nose at them and have a condescending attitude about their performance when, in fact, you are the one who can't perform anywhere near their level, then ultimately, you have lost their respect and your credibility.

But suppose it is even worse than that. Let me tell you about a "leader" who showed up at the range on qualification day with his gut hanging so far over his belt his magazine pouches were bent outward. This leader hands his score sheet to the range officer who quickly writes down a passing score and the leader leaves the range without his handgun ever leaving its holster. What message did this "leader" (and the range officer) send to all the officers who just witnessed this? What standard was set by this leader? How would you rate this leader's moral fiber? Will these officers follow this leader into a bad situation? Would you? I just might follow him out of pure curiosity… I would be interested to see how this leader goes about his day. Many leaders who act like they deserve special rules (or that the rules don't apply to them) will bully their subordinates into submission, thereby stroking the fragile ego of these poor leaders. Self-serving versus selfless-service. You, as a leader, will never be above the law; at least not in a republic such as ours.

> Another commander who was in charge of our outfit had a pet peeve for uniforms and facial hair. He wanted everyone to be in the correct garrison uniform even when we were getting ready to assault. Garrison uniforms are not made for performance in the field. Field uniforms are not made for the parade field. They

are not pressed and have baggy pockets on the sleeves; the overall appearance is poor while the performance is high. This commander also did not care for the crazy facial hair that Special Operators seem to favor. I must admit that sometimes it was a little out of control. Our way of thinking was that if we needed it, we had it. If we didn't, we could shave it off. There are times when having facial hair is a must to blend in. The Middle East, the area of the world in which we were deployed during this time, is just such an area. So, we have a commander who didn't like out of regulation uniforms or facial hair. He despised the uniform and facial hair standards being bent to fit the mission even though the commanders before him had set the precedence that this diversion from the common military standards was needed in order to aid in the successful accomplishment of our mission. So this commander ranted and raved about our looks which had nothing to do with our performance or the specific mission at hand. He chose to enforce uniform policy but dismiss height and weight standards. Did I mention he was overweight? As a Special Operations soldier, you are expected to perform. If your weight does not allow you to maintain the required physical fitness standards, it will have detrimental effects on the mission at hand. This can also be an important fact if you become injured and your teammates have to carry you.

This commander, although not a bad guy, had lost credibility by picking and choosing the standards he would follow instead of following the same standards as his men. It can't be this way if you are to be respected and followed by your people. You, of all people, must stay on track and set the standard for performance, not just appearance. Who would you want fighting on the battlefield with you: the man who will perform or the man who will dress perfectly for the parade field but can't perform the mission or task at hand?

Your subordinates are smart people and you, as a leader, work for them. They see what is going on. They know there are standards they are required to maintain and they expect the same from you. As a leader you must be beyond reproach when it comes to standards.

As I said earlier, you don't have to be first, but don't be last. Maintain your level of proficiency no matter the task.

Lessons Learned

- You must live by the same standards as your men and women.
- Hold yourself to the same or higher standards as your men.
- One of the marks of a professional organization is that it has one set of rules for everyone, not one set of rules for the bosses and another set for the regular folk.

"A king does not abide within his tent while his men bleed and die upon the field. A king does not dine while his men go hungry, nor sleep when they stand at watch upon the wall. A king does not command his men's loyalty through fear nor purchase it with gold; he earns their love by the sweat of his own back and the pains he endures for their own sake. That which comprises the hardest burden, a king lifts first and sets down last. A king does not require service of those he leads but provides it to them. He serves them, not they him."

-- Steven Pressfield
Gates of Fire

CHAPTER 15
A LEADER'S COURAGE

Citation:
For extraordinary heroism in action on 26 April 2004, during combat operations against an armed Iraqi Insurgent force while supporting United States Marine Corps operations in Fallujah, Iraq. Staff Sergeant Briggs repeatedly subjected himself to intense and unrelenting enemy fire in order to provide critical medical attention to severely injured Marines and organized defensive operations. He set the highest example of personal bravery through his demonstrated valor and calmness under fire. Staff Sergeant Briggs' valiant actions prevented enemy insurgent forces from over-running the United States Force's position and were directly responsible for prevention of additional United States military casualties or Prisoners of War by the enemy. His actions under fire as a combat medic were performed with marked distinction and bravery. Staff Sergeant Briggs' distinctive accomplishments are in keeping with the finest traditions of the military service and reflect great credit upon himself, this command, and the United States Army.

This is the actual citation written on the Distinguished Service Cross that was awarded to SSG Dan Briggs. This is what *courage* is all about. Dan was a great medic and went on to become a great operator. This is an example of not only courage under fire but courageous leadership. The Marines in Fallujah that day looked to Dan for guidance. He set an example which some emulated with their actions during the Battle of Fallujah in 2004, while others simply chose to follow this courageous warrior.

Dan was later injured when a suicide bomber blew himself up during the conduct of combat operations. He continues to have regular surgeries to get his body put back into proper working order.

Leadership Courage

Being courageous as a leader isn't always about running into the gunfire. It is about standing up and being accountable for your actions or accountable for those around you. It is also important that you, as a leader, are not a crowd follower. They call you a leader for a reason. Step up and do it.

It is common for incompetent leaders to lack the courage to stand up to superiors when poor decisions are made. Having a lack of confidence in yourself will immediately put you behind the power curve when unqualified commanders or bosses hand down poor decisions. It only takes throwing your people under the bus a couple of times to lose all your credibility in the eyes of your subordinates. You should be a courageous leader who *always* stands up for what is right, not just when it is convenient.

You must build your credibility by getting the needed occupational training and experience to back up your decisions. You must courageously step out in front to lead your people. If you are not up to the task, let someone else who is ready to lead, lead. You won't always make perfect decisions, and from time to time you will stumble along the way. If you are giving it your all and making the necessary sacrifices, your people will appreciate the effort. As long as you learn from your shortcomings, you will be a better leader in the long run.

Courage isn't something that comes easily. You are going to be tempted to sit back and watch from the sidelines.

Military and Law Enforcement leaders must sustain their courage to do what is right; to lead when others have stopped. This could be the difference between life and death.

Business leaders must also have the courage to carry on in the right direction. The consequences may not seem as dire in the business world, but in the end, all leaders who stand up and make the hard decisions require courage.

Max Hastings, the author of *Inferno*, a great book on the history of WWII, quotes Luftwaffe NCO Walter Schneider: "Nobody has the courage to act in accordance with his natural cowardice with the whole company looking on."[1]

There is truth in Schneider's paradox. I know, as a Special Operations soldier, not having the "courage" to quit in front of others forced me to endure and finish many things I never thought possible. Luckily, I was not courageous when it came to being a quitter.

Lessons Learned

- Courage is not just about bravery on the battlefield. It is about being accountable at all times throughout your life.
- One of the greatest sources of courage can come from not wanting to disappoint those around you.

"When a warrior fights not for himself, but for his brothers, when his most passionately sought goal is neither glory nor his own life's preservation, but to spend his substance for them, his comrades, not to abandon them, not to prove unworthy of them, then his heart truly has achieved contempt for death, and with that he transcends himself and his actions touch the sublime."

-- Steven Pressfield
Gates of Fire

CHAPTER 16
BE RESPONSIBLE

"It's not my fault."

Is this a common mantra in your workplace? If it is, then look at those you lead and see if they are constantly shirking responsibility. If they are, then this may be a reflection of your leadership style. You must send the message to your people that taking responsibility for one's actions is the ***only*** acceptable course of action.

In this day and age of everyone else but little ol' me is responsible, you might have a tough road ahead. Nowadays it is very common for almost everyone you come in contact with to shift the blame on to others and not own up to their own shortcomings. As I said earlier, if you see this, you must stop it. You, as the leader, have to set the example. If you have made a mistake, own up to it; but only if you made the mistake. If subordinates made the mistake, point it out to them only if they don't come clean and take responsibility first. Pushing people to take responsibility shouldn't be an exercise in embarrassing or belittling them. You have to ease folks into this concept until they realize that when they screw up they learn from it and we all move forward in a positive manner.

An excellent way to do this is with a quick After Action Review (AAR). Once the operation is over, talk through it and have each individual point out shortcomings of the task or mission. As deficiencies are noted, make sure to indicate who was responsible for the shortcoming. At first, this will be incredibly hard for some to swallow, but if you can build a group that is focused on mission accomplishment and not on passing the buck or shifting the blame, you will have a very strong organization. The key is that everyone stands up for their actions.

During Operation Iraqi Freedom, several military police personnel at Abu Ghraib prison in Baghdad, Iraq were found to be using poor judgment in their interactions with terrorist prisoners. These misguided military personnel posed for pictures with prisoners while they were in demoralizing poses and undergoing what some would call torture. The discussion here is not whether the techniques used were torture or not. The discussion is about the lack of leadership in this facility.

When all was said and done, the two individuals lowest on the totem pole were punished while everyone in the chain of command played the blame game accusing those above and below but never stepping up and being accountable and responsible. This passing of the buck made it to the very top of our government personnel, yet no one took the responsibility.

What message has the military sent to all of its personnel? I would perceive it as this, "I am in charge, but not responsible."

Delegate authority not responsibility

In the US Army we often hear the saying, "you can delegate authority but not responsibility." After seeing the aftermath of Abu Ghraib, I guess this must be an empty statement. When it was all said and done, the subordinates were placed in prison like the terrorists they once guarded; but you have to have your head in the sand if you believe that no one other than those lowly few knew what was going on behind the bars of Abu Ghraib. If, like me, your eyes are wide open and you have a touch of common sense, you know leaders shirked their responsibilities.

This particular incident of failing to take responsibility had several layers of fallout. The first layer deals with the subordinates who stopped trusting their superior officers. You can't blame them for deciding they needed to cover their own butts after seeing what happened in this prison. What kind of work environment exists when the rank and file doesn't trust those in charge? Probably one in which mission accomplishment is not frequently achieved.

Next there is the issue of productivity in these prisons. High Value Targets (HVT) were held in detention at Abu Ghraib with the intention they would provide information so even more HVT's could be tracked down. When attention was focused on this facility because of the irresponsible actions of a few, it almost shut down the entire intelligence gathering effort. If prisoners are not being questioned, how will we gather the needed intelligence to find the top tier terrorists? This near breakdown in the intelligence gathering process occurred because leaders were afraid of doing what they are chartered to do; be responsible.

The final layer of fallout happened on the battlefield where the repercussions of this debacle were very vivid. Infantrymen were being investigated if they brought back a detainee from the battlefield that had any bruises or was bleeding. It didn't matter what Soldiers or Marines did in the heat of the moment in order to stay alive. There was a presumption of guilt placed on these warriors which forced them to justify, to an investigator's satisfaction, how an enemy terrorist was injured in combat. Innocent Soldiers were asked to enter buildings at night in order to arrest terrorists and then found themselves being interrogated by military officials about the mission with which they were just tasked. This is disturbing.

So, at the end of the day, we had a few people entertained by taking pictures with terrorists, leaders who failed to stand up in order to stop the circus, and, instead, let it get out of control. After it was completely out of control, they still did nothing. Even after charges were filed, the leaders continued to plead ignorance. This is a pathetic example of leadership. Sadder, is the fact that no one took responsibility.

The incident in Abu Ghraib had more negative downstream effects than anything else that has happened during the Global War on Terror (GWOT). This event took away our war fighters' ability to hunt down and destroy terrorist networks. Young men and women were being investigated at the drop of a hat while the terrorists they arrested enjoyed orange juice, hot meals, and showers.

Take the lessons of Abu Ghraib to heart. If you fail to stand up and take responsibility when you should, the consequences of your failure will ripple throughout your entire organization, magnifying the damage far beyond the original issue at hand. The impact you have on your organization, whether military or business, is incredible. You are the one who is leading, which puts you in the critical position of being where the rubber meets the road. If you study any failures, you can always attribute these to leadership. So before you take the pay raise or increased responsibility, ask yourself if you are ready for the heat that comes with it. There is no doubt you will experience failure. How will you, as a leader, deal with that failure? Will you let it define you or will it make you more resilient for the next challenge? Down the road, when the next challenge presents itself, your past failures will be a source of experience from which to draw. This will help to improve your future decisions. Failure is a great facilitator for learning and improvement.

Strong leaders answer the mail. They get their people back on track and power straight ahead into the next round of adversity.

Don't underestimate the power of your position. You have the weight of responsibility on your shoulders. You cannot let your people down. Stand up and lead. If you *delegate authority*, be very aware that you are still ultimately *responsible*.

Lessons Learned

- You are responsible.
- Failing to take responsibility will lead to mission failure and, possibly, the destruction of your entire organization.
- Delegate authority but continue to be responsible.

CHAPTER 17
ACCOUNTABLE LEADERS

It's your fault!

If you have a failure in your organization, you as a leader are at fault. Don't pass the buck, own up to your shortcomings. This isn't intended to sound harsh; however it is just a fact that is often overlooked. We have people in our organizations that fail, they misstep and fall on their face. We as leaders should be there to pick them up and help all that are involved in order to learn from these mistakes.

A large portion of what it means to be accountable is simply being present for your people. If they need you, you should be easily accessible. If you are accessible for making timely decisions and take an active role in the professional development of your leadership staff, they will use you for guidance when needed. If you give sound and clear guidance, your people will have a better idea of where you stand on specific issues instead of running around guessing what you will think of this or that.

Don't sugar coat it

If one of your leaders screws up, they need to be immediately accountable for their actions. It is best to just call a spade a spade. Don't sugar coat it. This is big boy business, with big boy rules, so act like one. Feelings will get hurt, but if you are truly in this to win, you should want the best for your organization. Sometimes feelings will need to be hurt to accomplish this task, so call it like you see it. This includes your own mistakes too.

After Action Review = Hotwash

> *In Special Operations organizations we use After Action Reviews (AAR's) or Hotwashes. A Hotwash takes place <u>immediately</u> after the action you are to critique. For example, if we cleared one room during training to work on a specific skill set, we Hotwashed the training immediately following the training iteration. After a while, this simple idea of critiquing your training will help during large, full-scale AAR's or debriefs, as they are called in some organizations.*

If you make it the standard to always discuss what happened, you will quickly see improvement. It is ok to go ahead and talk about what you did right but more importantly, you must get to the bottom of what you did wrong. This is when and where improvement will take place. You will also see that some in your group don't want to take ownership for inappropriate actions or poor performance. This is where we must teach them to understand that we are pointing out deficiencies in all that are involved in order to become a better team as a whole. One individual who cannot be critiqued without becoming offended is a problem. You, as a group, should work together to fix this problem. Speak openly with your team, let them know you are all in this together, but owning up to a shortcoming is a must if you want to see improvement. The trademark of a good team is one that can accept criticism together as a whole and move forward and fix the problems once they are brought to light.

CHAPTER 17 ACCOUNTABLE LEADERS

After our actions in the Streets of Mogadishu on 3 October 1993, there were some leaders in our chain of command that wanted to pass the buck or shy away from what really happened. Some simply wanted to forget about what happened even though this mission was a perfect opportunity from which to learn. There were lessons learned in Mogadishu that have saved countless number of lives during the Global War on Terror (GWOT).

When Lt. Tom D returned from Somalia, he wanted to pass on lessons learned to fellow Rangers and their leaders so they would not replicate the perceived shortcomings of the 3 October mission. He was told, by his company commander, that he would not be allowed to conduct this AAR and distribute the Lessons Learned to other Rangers. His company commander went so far as to remove him from a leadership position as a platoon leader and move him into the company executive officer position. In reality this is a promotion. Why would this happen? It is my belief that it happened because the company commander knew he would receive criticism for his actions, or lack of actions, in the streets of Mogadishu that day. Therefore, it would do less damage to his ego if the Lessons Learned were not allowed out. To put your ego or career ahead of a chance for your organization to learn new lessons and grow is unforgivable. Of course we don't need to dwell on the last battle, but we should glean as much information as we can from the AAR and learn from it, allowing us to prepare for the next battle.

The company commander is at fault in this particular case, but what about you? Are you constantly researching the past actions of organizations like yours? History must be studied or we will be destined to repeat the same mistakes. We can often avoid unforeseen mistakes by having historical knowledge from other organizations about which we have read or studied. We can avoid the pitfalls that others have stumbled into by studying our Country's history, reading stories of the battles that forged our Nation and its leaders, or simply by examining books about business leaders. All of these resources are great tools that we must use constantly to further our organization. Before Mogadishu, there were selection criteria in place that could have helped prevent some of that day's failures, specifically, the Ranger Orientation Program (ROP). However, some Ranger leaders who did not pass ROP were still allowed to take command, thereby demonstrating a lack of accountability on the part of their superiors. (See the Selecting Leaders & Standards Chapters for more information about ROP.)

SFC Jon H, my team leader, was always accountable as a leader. If we performed, he put us on a pedestal. If we failed, he stepped forward and took the blame. He knew training the team to perform was his responsibility. He also knew any failures were due to his leadership. Is this a harsh statement? Absolutely not. It is this attitude that you must possess in order to make more leaders step up and be accountable for their actions and the actions of their team. Even if Jon wasn't responsible, he stepped up to show his men that he was there to help them attain the goals they set. And yet, just another reason he is a great leader.

Lessons Learned

- You are accountable **for** your people.
- You are accountable **to** your people.

CHAPTER 18
BE APPROACHABLE

If you are like most people I know in leadership positions, you are limited only by your lack of understanding of the situation at hand. If you had the ability to analyze your actions after the fact, you would undoubtedly be able to find some constructive criticism for yourself. That is, if you are truly honest with yourself. So, as you look back on your previous experiences, what would you like a "Mulligan" or a do over on? Would it be the way you treated those who serve you? Were you engaged enough with your people? Did you provide enough mentorship? How about to your leaders? Were you able to be spoken to without issue? Were the discussions tense and one-sided or were they easy going and two-way?

I have seen many leaders who look down on those they lead. Some leaders see their people as a bother or an annoyance. They feel they are better than anyone else in the vicinity simply because they have ended up in a leadership position. There are situations where this may be true but, more than likely, it is just the opposite. Chances are you have folks working with and for you who are more intelligent than you. Or, if they are not more intelligent, they may have a skill set that you don't have in your repertoire.

Some leaders take this condescension a step further and act like bullies towards their people. If you are a bully leader, it is really hard for people to feel comfortable talking to you.

If this is the case, you will never get the real perspective on those you are leading. I feel sorry for you because these are the people who can make you successful if you would just take a minute to listen to what they have to say. After knowing a bully leader for a while, I normally find out they are compensating for one or more of their own shortcomings with their hardcore treatment of their people. By being unapproachable and harsh, they hope to keep their own inadequacies hidden from everyone around them. Even worse, there are cases where someone who was treated like crap by their leader goes on to a leadership position themselves and repeats the same destructive behavior because he or she believes it to be the norm. Well, it is definitely not the norm for a great leader. Unfortunately, the behavior of one bully leader like this can spread through an organization like cancer if it isn't stopped.

There are times when leaders can't be approachable. One of those times is when military leaders are on the battlefield. The heat of the battle is not the time to have a sit down discussion with one of your subordinate commanders. During battle it should be all business; figuring out if you will follow your plan or deviate from that plan. Discussions with subordinates about the plan and contingencies may be a different story. If there are changes that need to be made, you must get input from those who have a better awareness or understanding of the battlefield than you do. Contingencies must be addressed as well, since they may be time sensitive.

There is another facet to being approachable which you must consider. I hear many leaders say they have "an open door policy." I have no doubt that most of them are being 100 percent sincere when they say this, but they are overlooking one critical point: They are still the boss. Some subordinates (especially new ones) may be too intimidated to actually approach their superior in his or her office. So you, as a leader, must go to them, at least initially. Meet your people where they work or in a common area in order to put them at ease. Once you establish your approachability to your people, they'll know they can come to you when needed.

Paralysis through analysis

There are also times when discussions do nothing but waste your time. If this is the case, you need to start having discussions with different people at work. Some of your subordinates want to talk with you just for face time and not accomplish anything. You need to figure this out quickly and line them out (sorry, have to throw some cowboy jargon at you every now and then…it means to get them in order, organized) so they understand you need to walk away from conversations smarter and not feel like you wasted your time.

Who are you and what are your strengths?

It is always fun to sit down with a new soldier and get to know them. We can find out what a new soldier has done from their personnel file, but what really makes them tick? What are their likes and dislikes? What are their political and religious views? Yes, I know, these are two subjects we should never discuss. That is, unless you are serving beside one another on the battlefield or as members of a small team where team dynamics play a vital role to your survival. You need to know everything you can about your soldiers. It could save your life. Additionally, it is important to get to know what these soldiers are dealing with at home because that key piece of info can have good and bad results when deployed or operational.

Getting to know the soldier, and his or her family and situation, is important. More importantly, you need to figure out the strengths and weaknesses of this soldier. What skill sets do they bring to the table which can enhance your team?

In Special Operations, language skills are important. It can be a key factor when figuring out who will deploy where.

I always enjoyed seeing what people have as a passion. My old mate, George H., had a love for languages. As a kid working at a Chinese restaurant, he learned to speak Mandarin Chinese. That is an amazing feat in itself. At that point in his life he realized he enjoyed learning to speak any language which may help him out. Over the course of his military career, he learned to speak at least five languages and I am sure he continues to dabble even today as a retired soldier. Not only did he learn the languages, he used them to enhance the mission at hand. No matter where we were deployed he would tune up on their language, immerse himself, and make a difference.

The bottom line is there are many positive things which can come from being approachable. You will learn about your people. You can gain their trust so, in times of crisis, they will seek you out for advice. They will look to you as a mentor when making career decisions. It is also a way for you to figure out who should move up the ladder into positions of increased responsibility.

Don't sit down and be patronizing with these great individuals who work for you, they deserve better.

You will also be able to develop a guideline as to how this person likes to be led. What are the most important leadership traits to this person? Do you have those traits? What type of leaders has this man or woman had in the past and how did that work out? You have so many things to learn as you sit across from someone you don't know. Be sure you don't dominate the conversation with your stories and pontification. Let them tell you some stories and what they see as important in the world.

Sit down and glean as much information as you can and then put it to use building your unstoppable team.

Lessons Learned

- If your people feel they can't come to you with a problem, you've already failed as a leader.
- Leaders must understand that each and every person on their team has something of value to offer. It's the leader's job to figure out just what that "something" is.

"To be humble to superiors is duty, to equals courtesy, to inferiors nobleness."

-- Ben Franklin

CHAPTER 19
MOTIVATION

There are folks I have met who are very motivated by money and status. If you are one of these individuals, please take a minute and consider where you have gone wrong. True motivation does not come from money or fancy titles. In fact, true motivation can be free and using it in your organization is only one leadership decision away.

We all need cash to survive; it is just a fact of life. However, money doesn't motivate the talented people in most industries. So, let's get past using bribes to get folks to work. Of course there should be an incentive for your people, whether they are in a business or in the military, to work hard and possibly get a bonus. The catch is, the military doesn't have bonuses. Unless you consider not getting killed and completing a mission that has positive effects for people around the world a bonus. I do.

As I reflect on some of the great leaders whom I had the honor of serving, I think about the ways they motivated their teams. Whether they were military or business leaders, they used similar methods.

Ownership

A simple technique that works extremely well (and is free) is to give your subordinates *ownership*. Whatever the task, passing responsibility onto your people will increase their motivation. Even when you have slow or substandard performers, they will rise to the occasion and get the job done when they are put in charge. Why do they do this? Is it for personal gain or is it to show you they can get things done if you only give them a chance? Hopefully it is the latter. Even if it isn't, they may learn how great it feels to have accomplished something while at the helm and seek out opportunities to be in charge of even more projects. This is motivating. Everyone deep down wants to be successful, and once they get a taste of it they will want more. The trick is for you to do two things: First, put these people in charge of the project and then supervise without being condescending. Second, let them do it their way, don't micromanage. There is a difference between micromanaging and supervising. Always remember, you are the leader and you still retain overall responsibility.

Competition

My Team Leader, Jon H, is a competitive person. He constantly wanted us to perform at the highest level possible. So, to inspire us to perform, he used competitions. These competitions were not always about shooting or running. There were thinking competitions too. By having us solve problems together, we could start to see our teammates' strengths and weaknesses.

> One of our platoon competitions was performed in our swimming pool. The team had to complete a series of tasks, similar to a relay race. One of the tasks was to swim to the bottom of the 18-foot pool and blow bubbles into a military water can until it floated to the surface. For those of you that have not seen one of these, they look a lot like a plastic gas can but are meant for water. This water can was tied with a section of cord to a 45-pound plate from the gym. I thought to myself, "No problem, how hard can this be?" When it was my turn, I dove into the pool,

CHAPTER 19 MOTIVATION

swam down to the can, placed my lips by the cap, and blew a bubble the size of a pea into the can. This was completely ineffective in terms of accomplishing the mission of making the can float. Once I surfaced, my other teammates continued to swim down and blow air into the can. Eventually, there was enough air in the can to lift the 45 lb. plate to the surface. However, this was in no way due to any of my contributions during the competition. So, was I a failure? I would have been if I had said I can't do it. More importantly, it showed I had a glaring weakness to the rest of my team. I am not aqua man. Swimming isn't an issue, but I was not comfortable in this situation. I was embarrassed of course but, worse yet, I had let my team down and I wanted to remedy this situation in the worst way. My teammates, with guidance from our team leader, helped me with my water skills until raising a weighted can from the deep end of the pool, or any other crazy skill that might someday save a mate's life, wasn't a problem.

Simple competitions are the key. Use small, bite size chunks to see how your people perform. Their motivation will rise as long as you focus these competitions on each team members' skill set. If you want a well-rounded team working for you, then use well-rounded competitions.

Team Effort

This story describes how teamwork inspired a weak link (that would be me) to perform better during an intimidating task. If you, as a leader, can get your people to work as a team, life will be great. Teamwork sounds easy, but many times it takes serious trial and error to get everyone to work together. Just because you say you're a team doesn't magically make it happen. You have to work with your team to show them what this really means. Being a team is more than working together on a project for a few hours. If you are on a team, you need to build a bond with the rest of your team. Not as easy as it sounds when we all have differing views, opinions, and life experiences. You may also have to deal with distractions outside of work; inevitably there is always someone who wants to get off work to hang out with the family or girlfriend. I see these distractions as two types, frivolous and real. The family being real, the girlfriend being frivolous. That is until the girlfriend becomes serious enough to make it a real distraction. Your team may have different levels of education. You may have academics that will show their strengths for one problem yet, during the next go around of tasks, those with experience are needed to step up and solve an issue while the academics remain in a supporting role. A team succeeds together, but it must fail together too. This will only make the team stronger in the long run.

Mission Focus

Having a mission or goal is an easy way to motivate your mates. If you have given clear guidance on what you want the end state to be, step back and let your subordinates get after it. It is very inspiring to brief your team on the mission then watch them problem solve until reaching a final solution. Not only will you have a motivated team, you will be able to see who has what strengths.

A mission statement is a way to focus your team each day and remind them why they are doing what they do. Every member of your team, not just the leaders, needs to know and understand this mission statement.

Dial in

Find out your people's passions. Once you know what makes them hungry to perform, what makes their hearts pound harder, you will be able to focus their strengths and passions on the mission. When a leader understands where the members of his team are coming from, he can use their strengths to improve the whole team. I have seen some people who obsess over certain aspects of their job or even a job related hobby. You need to capitalize on this fire.

Attaboys

Attaboys are words of encouragement. This is extremely important to some people. Certain folks need encouraging words and, as their leader, the task of handing out these attaboys falls directly on your shoulders. It is simple, quit being negative and give your people some positive reinforcement. It won't hurt, I promise. This shouldn't have to be discussed but, too often, I see leaders who only complain and chastise their teams. You will accomplish absolutely zero with this technique. More important, if all you do is complain, eventually your team will completely tune you out. I get it; there are times when we need to chew some tail. But that should not be the norm. For example, "Hey, today your performance was not awesome!" See how positive that sounds! Just kidding. Give folks a pat on the back when they need it and, especially, when they deserve it.

Periodic Review or Performance Counseling

Some would say counseling is not perceived as a motivator, but I would disagree. Some performers are truly motivated by continued higher performance standards, as crazy as a thought process as that sounds. What better way to perform than to be told what is expected, where they stand and how they can take it to the next level? Performers are not stymied by performance analysis and feedback. They want to constantly strive to please their leaders, improve their work, and complete another mission.

Knowing your people and knowing what motivates them is key. Every individual you lead is unique. The methods with which you motivate them must also be unique. It is your job to figure this out and rise to the occasion. You won't be disappointed. Find a way to motivate all of those who serve you in their own way.

Lessons Learned

- Find people's strengths and capitalize on them.
- Find people's weaknesses and improve them, as a team.

CHAPTER 20
EARNING MENTALITY

Status and Entitlement vs. Merit and Productivity

Status and Entitlement

Status and entitlement are alive and well. Our country is being destroyed by this entitlement mentality. We have so many people who feel *we* owe *them*. For what? First off, how did I become part of *we* and not part of *them*? I work hard, earn my money, and have fought my way to becoming successful. For this I should owe those who feel entitled to part of my success? Wrong. That is as far from being an American as you can possibly be. It seems the new American Dream is to get as much free stuff as you can with as little effort as possible. That mentality is just not sustainable.

Now apply this same thinking to your organization. You feel you are entitled to a promotion simply because of time on the job or maybe because of your status in this business? This is not sustainable either. Your organization needs you to produce. Not produce once and live on that past, outdated performance. But produce on a daily basis that continually pushes your organization towards mission accomplishment.

Merit and Productivity

Now for the other side of the coin: If you have a group of individuals with merit, they have earned it. They worked hard to earn it. They didn't just meet some time standard for being on the job. Another important piece of trivia is that they were working while they were on the job, not just biding their time. Do you feel good about selecting this individual for advancement based on their merit and productivity? Absolutely.

We need producers. These are the folks getting the job done on a daily basis. They *earn* their paycheck, not once, but each and every week. These are the individuals who should be pushed into positions of greater responsibility when they are ready.

Developing the Earning Mentality

You as the leader must ensure that the earning mentality is rewarded. If you pander to the less-than-motivated, it will continue to pull your organization down. Push your people to perform. Not on a semiannual basis, but every chance you get. Never stop pushing for performance.

A common quote from fellow Special Operations soldiers was, "I have never worked so hard to be mediocre!"

Every day was a new event with all of the Special Ops soldiers working as hard as possible to keep their spot on the team. You couldn't stumble for worry of being passed by a man with more hunger for success than you. These are the kinds of attitudes we want to reward, striving for success. In these units, success is mission accomplishment.

Mission Accomplishment

How would it work in the military world if a mission were handed down that requires sacrifice, but no one wants to participate because it demands work, sweat, and many hours without sleep? When you do get to sleep it's cold and wet and, more than likely, on the ground. Of course, the other possibility is that you might be called to make the ultimate sacrifice... to give your life for your mates on your left and your right, for your country.

Those that believe in *status and entitlement* will definitely not want to be involved in this mission. Why would they want to make a sacrifice, to be miserable, when someone will always take care of them? You have seen this attitude.

In US Army Special Operations there isn't a lot of the entitlement attitude, at least not in the younger soldiers. I must say, I have seen a few old dogs that think they have made it. Not the right approach to take in this business. Having the arrogance to believe you don't have to prove yourself anymore will help you quickly lose any remaining credibility that you may have earned in the past.

These Special Operations soldiers constantly strive to make life better, not only for their fellow soldiers, but for everyone with whom they come in contact. Their daily grind isn't a grind at all; it is a chance to make a difference. Not only is that the correct attitude for followers, but leaders can also set the example for their people by truly having a *merit and productivity* based mindset.

As Americans we often think we are so different than others on this planet. I would whole-heartedly disagree. Warriors around the world have an interestingly similar mindset. Even our Cold War enemies feel that they can make a difference if they strive to perform for their fellow comrades.

As the Russian Special Forces un-official slogan says:

"Yesle nye ya, to kto!"

"If not me, then who?"[1]

As a leader, you should constantly strive to make that difference. No matter what position you are currently in, if you go into work each and every day with a *producing* attitude, you will help make your team successful. Help carry the load, don't be a burden to your team.

> *Even our kids love competition; they want to perform, to do better than those around them. So what do we do in today's society? We punish those that perform by minimizing their efforts and elevating the non-performers to the same level as the hard working children. This is wrong and we all must work to fix this broken thinking. If we don't remedy the situation while our kids are young, they will be doomed to a life of Status and Entitlement; and I, for one, do not want that for my offspring. I want kids that are fighting every day to be at the top of the food chain.*

This newfound mission accomplishment, or earning mentality must come from the top in your organization and your family. Slackers beware if you think you are on easy street. We will pass you up, we will take your job, and we will finish ahead of you in this real world competition called life.

Lessons Learned

- Status and entitlement have no place in successful organizations.
- What have you earned today?

CHAPTER 21
CREDIBILITY

If you refer back to *Chapter 6: Leadership Traits in One Word*, you will remember my leadership word is *credibility*. Once again, this is not the only word you can choose as a defining leadership trait, but I feel it is very important. Credibility goes a long way in the leadership world. Actually, it goes a long way in anything you do in this world. There is a difference between credibility and reputation. Reputation is what others say about you, their opinions and their beliefs. Your credibility is the quality of being trusted and believed or simply, being worthy of trust.

Since I retired and started a business in the outdoor industry, I worked to develop a credible business relationship with our customers. Initially this was a simple task because every customer we had we already knew personally from either the military or the shooting community. After a while we started to grow and as we did, we had to work hard to develop and sustain credibility with our new customers. Credibility is a truth. It comes from within. In today's world of social media, a reputation can be obliterated with a few clicks of the keyboard; there is only so much you can do about it. Your credibility, however, lies within you. Your trustworthiness, believability, capability are truths which you know. Your credibility will manifest itself through your word, deeds and actions.

Now I understand the business world much better and it really isn't any different than the military. There I would establish my credibility on one team but if I moved to another, or had new team members come on board, I had to reestablish my credibility in order to gain their respect. The truth is I have always worked hard to establish my credibility each and every day.

As a SOF leader I was able to show new soldiers that credibility, and all that it stands for, isn't just handed out, it is earned each and every day. Many soldiers had glowing past performances in previous units but, if you didn't show the team what you had to offer *today*, what good would you be. As a business owner you will be much more successful if you try to build your own credibility rather than tear down others, I learned this the hard way. Today, I concentrate on building my own credibility and have stopped worrying about my competitors. It will all shake out in the end.

Leaders often stumble when they build their credibility to a certain level and then, once the tank is full, drive forever without refilling. This is absolutely wrong and you will soon be running on fumes. Your credibility must be built every hour of every day and it is built by serving those you lead. Make good decisions, be accountable, and lead. Every. Single. Day. Some of your decisions may not be popular but as long as they're the right ones, made for the right reasons, the team will succeed.

During the Battle of Mogadishu, our commander was named General William Garrison. We all called him "Wild Bill" Garrison. He was a gangly Texan who always had a cigar in his mouth. Not a dainty little cigar like you would see in an artsy black and white French film, but a full size dog turd cigar. He was always chewing on this no matter what time of day you caught him. General Garrison had served in the Special Operations community for many years. He stayed for an extended tour as our Unit commander when the right person could not be found to replace him. He did this even though it meant the destruction of his own career. Telling your leaders you don't want to move on doesn't go over well in the General Officers' world. Lucky for us who served with him, his decision to stay only helped make our Unit even stronger; and, contrary to what the rest of the General Officers' world thought, it built his credibility to an all-new high.

After the first mortar attack by the local terrorist clan on our compound in Mogadishu, General Garrison stood calmly in front of the task force and told us they were just "piddly little mortars" and we were not going to sit idly by while these terrorists did this to us. Later that night, we launched our first assault on the bad guys, hoping to send a clear message. I'm not sure if we sent a message to the bad guys but General Garrison sent a clear message to those that followed him: We could look to him as a credible, reliable leader who had our best interests in mind.

After the events of 3 October 1993 had transpired, there were all kinds of blame throwing going on. In the midst of all of this, General Garrison wrote a letter to those above him in the chain of command. How would you feel towards this man if he was your leader? I can tell you that we, as a task force, believe that General Garrison is a credible leader. A leader who, in this time of hardship, earned credibility by being accountable for his actions and those he led in Mogadishu.

In a hand written letter sent to Congressman John Murtha, here are General Garrison's own words. This wasn't a computer generated document but written by his own hand.

Congressman Murtha

Please show this to President Clinton and Sec. Aspin: I request that you not make it a public document.

Operation on 3-4 Oct '93 in Mog.

1. The authority, responsibility, and accountability for the Op rests here in MOG with the TF Ranger Commander, not in Washington.

2. Excellent intelligence was available on the target.

3. Forces were experienced in area as a result of six previous operations.

4. Enemy situation was well known
   • Proximity to Bakara Market (SNA Strong Point)
   • Previous reaction times of bad guys

5. Planning for Op was bottom up not top down. Assaulters were confident it was a doable operation. Approval of plan was retained by TF Ranger Commander.

6. Techniques, tactics and procedures were appropriate for mission/target.

7. Reaction forces were planned for contingencies
   • CSAR on immediate standby. (UH-60 with medics and security)
   • Ranger Co(-) as ground reaction force in armored HUMVEES

- 10th MTN Div QRF (coordinated with) (not organic)

8. Loss of 1st Helo was supportable. Pilot penned in wreckage presented problem.

9. 2'd Helo crash required response from 10th MTN QRF. The area of the crash was such that the SNA was there nearly immediately so we were unsuccessful in reaching the crash site in time.

10. Rangers on 1st crash site were not pinned down. They could have fought their way out. Our creed would not allow us to leave the body of the pilot penned in the wreckage.

11. Armor reaction force would have helped out casualty figures may or may not have been different. The type of men in this task force simply would not be denied in their mission of getting their fallen comrades.

12. The mission was a success. Targeted individuals were captured and extracted from the target.

13. For this particular target, President Clinton and Sec. Aspin need to be taken off of the blame line.

William F Garrison
MG
Commanding[1]

This document is unbelievably powerful especially when taken in the context of today's world of passing the buck. General Garrison stands up quickly in the very first paragraph.

> *"The authority, responsibility, and accountability for the Op rests here in MOG with the TF Ranger Commander, not in Washington."*

He takes responsibility for his and his men's actions. He doesn't try to make excuses. He comes right out and says that he is the one to look at if you have a problem. General Garrison is an *accountable* leader. In fact, this is one of the finest examples I've personally witnessed of a high level leader being accountable for his actions.

He continues taking responsibility with paragraph number five.

> *"Planning for Op was bottom up not top down. Assaulters were confident it was a doable operation. Approval of plan was retained by TF Ranger Commander."*

Once again, he tells those in Washington, D.C. exactly what happened. The mission was planned by his men; however, approval of the plan was retained by the Task Force Commander, which was General Garrison. This is a fine example of a leader delegating authority to those under his command and allowing them to do it their way while he constantly supervised. However, he understood that he was still responsible at the end of the day.

Of course, you can also read lucky number 13 and see why this document was, in fact, made public. It removes any blame from those in the highest government positions. When we compare the government officials at the time to General Garrison, we see a stark contrast of leadership styles. General Garrison did not shirk responsibility nor try to protect himself at the expense of those under his command. He stood up and held himself accountable thereby earning the respect and honor of all of his men. General Garrison is a *credible* leader.

If you aspire to be a great leader, credibility should be high on your list of leadership traits to acquire. This trait won't come easily and it can be lost in a second if you don't stay on your toes and always remain a leader. A poor decision, or poor treatment of your people, can have disastrous consequences to your credibility. Credibility in the eyes of those around you has a shelf life, so you need to make sure you add to it daily or it will sour.

Accountability came first. General Garrison was accountable for the actions of himself, his command, and his men. For this, he was given an immense amount of credibility, which has withstood the test of time.

Lessons Learned

- Credibility has a shelf life and must be renewed often.
- Being accountable is a great way to build your credibility.
- Great leaders have credibility as a key leadership trait.

THE MISSION

CHAPTER 22
DEFINING THE MISSION

What is your mission?

One of the core imperatives of leadership is to *accomplish the mission*. If the mission is unclear or, even worse, unknown, the chances of accomplishing it are close to zero. Given this, the ability of a leader to select, define, and then refine his mission is critical. A leader needs to explain the mission in a manner so those who work for him or her can easily understand it.

If you are a subordinate leader, you still must clearly understand the mission at hand. You may not have the ability to define and refine this mission but you will need to clearly explain the critical points to those you lead: what is expected by your higher leaders and how you plan to execute this mission.

Everyone has goals that they want to achieve so they can move further along the path to success. But these goals are not necessarily the mission. Goals are typically tasks or specific events that people want to accomplish at the end of the day. The mission is something larger; it is the overarching place where we want our organization to be when the dust settles.

If you live in an "in-extremis environment" on a daily basis, your mission may be different than a business leader. When I ask cops and military leaders what their mission is, I almost always get this answer: "I want all of my people to go home at the end of the day." This is an end state that briefs well and most of your superiors want this as well. I would go out on a limb and say that the average law abiding citizen wants the same thing for you. But is this a realistic mission to have as a law enforcement or military leader? As a member of the military or law enforcement, you operate in an environment in which the public has been told you will "Support and Defend," "Protect and Serve," or "Defend against all enemies, foreign and domestic." So where does, "I want all of my people going home at night," fit into your job description? Is that really your *mission*?

Now, before you get all bent out of shape, let me ask you a simple question: If a call comes over the radio that there is an Active Shooter killing innocent children in one of your local schools, what are you going to do? I really hope your answer is to drive there as fast as possible, run inside, and stop the killing at all costs. When the school shooting in Newtown, CT took place, there were off duty cops who ran into the school without weapons. They were prepared to do whatever they could with their bare hands. This was unbelievable courage and commitment on their part. Others who were carrying carbines handed these brave souls their pistols so they were able to have a weapon with which to fight.

Now that I have presented the situation from a slightly different perspective, do you still feel your primary focus should be on all of your people going home at the end of the night? I hope not. This is absolutely a desirable outcome, but it cannot be your core mission. If the officers at Newtown, CT had it as their mission, they would never have run into that school. If General Eisenhower had elevated the safety of his troops above his mission, America and the rest of the world would be a different place today. Assuming America still existed.

The above example demonstrates how a goal can sometimes be confused with the *mission*. Have you told your people the only important thing to you is that they all go home? If it is, you need to reassess your situation and truly tell those who look to you as a leader what you expect of them.

So, what is your *mission*?

Mission Accomplishment

Now that you have defined your mission, it is time to get to work accomplishing it.

Mission accomplishment should, and must be, your number one leadership goal. No matter what you do, regardless of your occupation, you must focus on your mission. Many leaders have forgotten this basic leadership goal. They have been elevated into a bureaucratic position which doesn't allow them to properly see the task at hand. They are more worried about mitigating risk than punishing the deserving. If you are not catching criminals and terrorist with every means at your disposal, you have lost your mission focus.

Please bear in mind I was a Sergeant Major who focused on assaulting numerous objectives weekly and sometimes numerous objectives in a 24-hour period. I was operating at the *tactical level*, not the *strategic level*. I am strong when it comes to tactics. Strategic or political thinking was not in my job description. There are reasons, I am sure, for certain decisions to be made. Ultimately though, military commanders must answer for their men and the mission at hand.

> We had a general in northern Iraq who wanted to "win Hearts and Minds" more than "Punish the Deserving." He couldn't understand how his

men were being wounded and killed during the most innocent of raids. He required his men to use a procedure employed in the United States by law enforcement officers: knock and announce. Soldiers were required to knock on the door of a known terrorist and then announce that they were "Amriki Askari," American soldiers. As you can imagine, with all speed and surprise lost, many men in the 101st Airborne were wounded or worse because of this loss of focus on mission accomplishment. Additionally, on one occasion this general actually sent staff members to warn a Black Listed Individual that we were coming. There is more to that story but suffice to say, we were lucky no one was wounded in the ambush set for us on that particular day at that particular target.

Six months later, the "Hearts and Minds" general had left and there was a new Sheriff in town in northern Iraq, Colonel Rounds. His unit's motto, "Punish the Deserving." The men and women of his brigade crushed the terrorist network and very rarely had American casualties. He is a man who understands Mission Accomplishment.

People are not the most important commodity. The <u>right</u> people are!

Once you understand that *mission accomplishment* is your most important leadership goal, you must *take care of the right people* along the way.

So, who are *the right people*?

Some leaders continue to chant the mantra "People are the most important thing in our business." This is true, if everyone is performing. But if not, then I would disagree. Some people are so bad it is actually like having two people working against you. If this is the case, you need to fix that problem.

Some of you may be unable to do this due to these problem people hiding behind their union membership. This is a common situation around the country. You have great performers and you have those who do only what their union rules require. The unfortunate actions of these few have a dumbing down effect on organizations and performance. These people are not the *right people*. They are not the folks who will accomplish your mission. They are hurting your team with their destructive behavior. There are times when unions are a good thing. Many law enforcement organizations have a police union because policemen are not taken care of by their city and their leaders. For example, if an officer needs representation after a shooting and his department won't provide it, he needs a policemen's organization to stand up for him. Unions should hold the performance of their members to the highest standards. It is up to the unions to police their own and keep non-performers from hiding under their protection.

Non-performers attract the attention of the leader because they are needy. They need training and mentoring to get them up to the desired level. But don't forget about those who are already performing for you every day. Don't overlook the performers who are getting it done. Take care of these people the same way you do the nonperformers.

Nonperformers often take the positive energy that is needed to keep our great performers moving. If that causes the high-energy guys to stagnate, you may lose all of your productivity. If the performers and producers are not mentored and continually trained, they might slide into the nonperformer column. That would be a travesty and you would be accountable for it. Push your people to perform; all of them. But don't spend all of your attention on the weak. You have performers who need to be taken care of and rewarded for their high level of performance. Those are the *right people*.

Mission Subversion and the Wrong People

I put "Defining the Mission" and "Taking Care of the Right People" in the same chapter because they are core elements of leadership. However, these two concepts can be easily perverted by unethical leaders and, as a result, cause great damage to an organization.

If an unethical leader is allowed free reign to define what the mission is going to be, it will have horrendous consequences on their organization. There is nothing to keep such a leader from defining the mission as "I need to be promoted," "I need to have my contract renewed," or "I need my next merit raise." None of those objectives are necessarily bad, but self-serving goals like these should never become the mission itself.

As one cop told me.

> "I witnessed one of my District Commanders say his #1 job every day was to make his boss, the Assistant Chief of Operations, "happy." He went on to say the #1 job of the three shift captains who worked for him was "to make him happy." The District Commander said this while teaching a Leadership & Ethics course to our department's personnel. He teaches the same course to every new recruit class at the police academy."

Imagine the damage this self-serving District Commander is inflicting on his department. To make matters worse, he will never be able to understand what is wrong with his mindset because having a good mission focus is beyond his comprehension. His mission is self-preservation and it is one which he has ingrained in himself and others for years.

"Taking care of the right people" can also become an excuse to justify bad leadership if used in an unethical manner. When the definition of "the right people" changes from the performers to a leader's softball team buddies, there is a huge problem.

A more serious misuse of this concept occurred at a police department where there had been a series of police involved shootings. Certain factions within the community were upset with the police so the department brought in outside agencies to investigate all of the deadly force encounters. In the end, these outside agencies found all the shootings to be completely justified. However, the police department never recognized the lifesaving actions of their officers who were involved in these critical incidents…with one exception. Two officers, who were good friends with uppermost management, were awarded their department's highest commendation. Did these officers deserve this award? Absolutely. They did an outstanding job. The unethical behavior surrounding this situation stems not from these officers but from the department's management who showed no regard for their rank and file officers but only those with whom they socialized.

What message did management send to the rank and file officers with this action? Did they *take care of the right people* or just their friends? Do you, as a leader, treat all of your people fairly or do you play favorites because of your personal relationships with some?

Both of these concepts, *Defining the Mission* and *Taking Care of the Right People*, are absolutely valid techniques but only if leaders use them in conjunction with moral fiber and integrity. If used unethically, these leadership principles will be twisted into self-serving rules.

Lessons Learned

- What is your mission?
- Define your mission carefully. This is not about you.
- Take care of the right people, not just your buddies.

CHAPTER 23
POLITICAL FOCUS OR MISSION FOCUS?

What is your focus?

When you roll out of bed in the morning, what is the plan for your day? Are you planning to focus on the mission at hand? The mission that every member of your task force or business is pushing towards? I call this *Mission Focus*. You have your eye on the prize and will work as hard as needed in order to get to the goal that you, or your higher leaders, have set. If you have your eye on the prize, and can keep everyone else focused in that direction too, you will be successful. Your junior leaders will know exactly what the end state is and everyone will be striving to attain that goal. You have given your people a clear *Commander's Intent (see Chapter 24: Commander's Intent)* and sent them on their way. You understand the how, when, where, and why might be slightly different than what you would choose, but in the end, they will accomplish the mission. As a new leader, this can be difficult. If you have always been a doer, and the recent promotion forces you to lead and supervise, anticipate the need to adjust to your new role. It isn't an easy task to just monitor progress versus doing. Just remember, your people are there to make all of you successful. Let them go and do great things. I call this technique *Mission Focus*.

Now on the other hand, you roll out of bed and immediately think about the best way to manipulate your way to the top or from whom you need to gather some "career nectar." If these are your first thoughts of the day, then you are not the mission-focused leader about whom I just spoke. All too often *Political Focus* becomes the strongest goal for your organization.

You will undoubtedly get sick of hearing me say that leadership is to blame when something bad happens. But, it is the truth. If you study the career of a military or business leader who has failed, you will undoubtedly discover that moment in time in which their failure was foreshadowed. I am an ardent believer in this theory; a theory which does not stem from academics but, instead, is rooted firmly in reality.

Many times over the last 30 years, I have examined situations and wondered why certain decisions were made. Whether it was the selection of a certain kid to be the starter for a football team or the selection of an individual to be a high-ranking military leader, I started to see certain trends. As a junior Noncommissioned Officer (NCO) in the military, I noticed that the strongest of the strong selected subordinates who, sometimes, broke a few windows on the way to accomplishing their mission. On the other hand, I saw the less talented leaders among the hierarchy (otherwise known as "the weak") select subordinates who would perform like puppets on a string.

After retiring from the Army, I spent a good portion of my time providing training to law enforcement professionals in the areas of firearms, tactics, and leadership. While I was with these officers, I started to recognize an all too familiar trend in struggling departments. Now don't get me wrong, there are some departments and cities that have it all figured out. Strong leaders abound when you have talent at the top. Other cities, however, are lucky they have cops on the streets that have not been infected by the sickness that has infested their brass. A sickness that causes these supposed police leaders

CHAPTER 23 POLITICAL FOCUS OR MISSION FOCUS?   119

to add levels of mission-killing bureaucracy and throw their support behind the criminals instead of their own officers. I know this is a strong statement, but I truly care about those cops who, every day, fight in the streets to bring bad guys to justice and do so with little to no support from their superiors. One minute, these crime fighters face disenfranchisement by their own captains and lieutenants who have turned their backs on justice in order to embrace the self-serving ethical code of career advancement; while in the next minute, they are confronted by a chief and mayor who's actions lead their officers to feel unsupported.

Those police leaders are not consciously listening to the criminal element, but they are engaging in knee-jerk reactions in response to the loudest sections of society, political opposition, media, and career special interest groups. These groups do not necessarily represent true public opinion or the law for that matter.

At its coarse fundamental core, the sickness poisoning American law enforcement's leadership is mere selfishness. There are some in leadership positions today who became officers with the promise they would put others before themselves but now put themselves, and their careers, ahead of all else. They disregard not only their promise, but their mission and the men under their command. Instead, their every waking moment is spent seeking out political favor from those in the community who will urge City Hall to promote their new "cop buddy." If, along the way, a few rules need to be bent, or their integrity tarnished further, it is but a small price to pay for that next promotion. Though few in number, self-serving malicious leaders like these inflict massive damage to their organizations. Unfortunately, this sickness is destroying American law enforcement in some places across the country and this nation's citizens are, in the end, the ones who will pay the price.

Perhaps this sickness is poisoning more of America's leaders than just those in law enforcement.

Let's look at law enforcement some more. There are times when the politicians appointed above you are running for reelection. During these times, you may see a completely different side of these individuals. They are out to appease those in their communities who make the most noise. And who might that be? Normally, the squeaky wheels are not the law-abiding pillars of your society. The squeakers are the controversial members of your community who have an axe to grind while they attempt to steer you in their direction. Here is an example:

Cha-Ching City, U.S.A.

The politicians at city hall decided it was easier to turn their backs on their own law enforcement professionals than to fight the criminals in their town. Anytime someone so much as hinted that they would sue the city for some sort of police action, the city rolled over and immediately paid the complainant some cash. So now you have a group of professionals that can't say "boo" without getting in trouble. Granted, if a cop is wrong, there should be reparations. But, if they were not, why should we pay off bad people with law-abiding taxpayers' cash?

In one particular case, the Metro SWAT Team was serving a warrant and entered the wrong building. When I say wrong building I mean they entered the building which they had a warrant for, signed by a

CHAPTER 23 POLITICAL FOCUS OR MISSION FOCUS?

judge, completely legitimate but an informant had sent them into a building adjacent to the actual drug dealer's house. There was nothing malicious about the entry, it was merely a mistake. What happened next is unbelievable. Inside this house, by chance, was a major criminal who had a warrant for murder. As the police entered, this criminal picks up a weapon to shoot the cops and the police kill the suspect. The city is sued by the suspect's relatives for killing their family member who was also in the United States illegally. The city doesn't miss a beat; they simply pay the family off and move on. There was no fault or premeditated plan to violate anyone's rights.

This is a fine example of *Political Motivation*. Why else would they simply hand over the money when their officers shot a bad man?

In America, we have a great system of checks and balances which was established by our Founding Fathers. We don't want bad cops running around terrorizing our society, so there must be safeguards in place. But, at the end of the day, law-abiding citizens need to stand up and get their local politicians to focus on what is important to their city. How has it become acceptable for bad men to get away with terrorizing civilians and cops? American politicians should be ashamed of themselves for letting this happen. If politicians are performing as needed but are being crucified by the media and a small contingent of opposing forces, we, as mainstream Americans, need to step up and stop letting this happen. Make a stand and support those in your community who are making the hard yet right decisions.

A leader holds to society's core values at all times, not just when it is politically convenient and easy.

Those from the business world are not immune to the mission destroying effects of political focus. This became very evident when I retired from the Army and began to consult for several large companies in the *Outdoor Industry*. Some were nimble and moved aggressively towards their company's goals. This allowed me to easily integrate into their company and help them strive to be the best they could be. This environment was similar to what I had grown accustomed to in the Special Operations community. It wasn't about personal goals in the Army; it was about the Unit's goals.

Other companies had become completely bureaucratic. Survival and self-promotion were the flavors of the day. Goals were set, but never met. Answers were given, but never truthful ones. Leaders were told what they wanted to hear, not what they needed to know. Almost every employee was running scared because of the threat that they would be fired if they made waves…or didn't make their numbers. I was of no service to anyone in this type of toxic corporate climate. How could I help with innovation or leadership when I couldn't get a straight answer or transition an idea through the bureaucracy? The leaders at the top of this business are the lucky few who can transform it back into a productive organization. To date, they have not made that transition. I am still hopeful that, one day, a truly great leader will take the helm and make this transformation.

Take a hard look at your organization. It doesn't matter if you work in the military, the government, or the civilian sector; you can make a difference by choosing the right path. Don't get lured into political and bureaucratic buffoonery. Give your team a mission, supervise, and watch them blow things off the chart. You will be able to stand back and be proud of what you have accomplished.

CHAPTER 23 POLITICAL FOCUS OR MISSION FOCUS?

Lessons Learned

- What is your focus? The mission or the politics of personal gain.
- Behind every failed organization you'll find a failed leader.

"Tiger, one day you will come to a fork in the road and you're going to have to make a decision about which direction you want to go.

"If you go one way you can **be somebody**. *You will have to make compromises and you will have to turn your back on your friends. But you will be a member of the club and you will get promoted and you will get good assignments.*

"Or you can go the other way and you can **do something** *– something for your country and for your Air Force and for yourself. If you decide you want to do something, you may not get promoted and you may not get the good assignments and you certainly will not be a favorite of your superiors. But you won't have to compromise yourself. You will be true to your friends and to yourself. And your work might make a difference.*

"To **be somebody** *or to* **do something**. *In life there is often a roll call. That's when you will have to make a decision. To* **be** *or to* **do**? *Which way will you go?"*

-- Colonel John Boyd

CHAPTER 24
COMMANDER'S INTENT

What the heck is *Commander's Intent*, and why would I want to apply this scary military term to my business or department?

Commander's Intent is the end state that your commander desires. It can be verbalized or written. End state means, after the mission is complete, what will have been accomplished. The *Commander's Intent* will help his unit, or subordinate units, focus their combat power to attain the end state. The importance of the *Commander's Intent*, from a purely practical view, is this: Here is what I want done at the end of the day. He or she is not telling you how to conduct that mission, or when, but what they want the battlefield to look like at its completion. Of course, you will have the occasional Micromanager-Commander who dictates the exact manner in which the end state will be reached. But this is not truly *Commander's Intent*. If you want to be successful as a leader, you must use the strengths of all of your assigned personnel. Not only will this make things go smoothly, but also you, as a commander, will be able to better facilitate the desired end state if you command and not micromanage. There are normally a few caveats to any *Commander's Intent*. There may be a desired line of attack or you may have adjacent units of which you must be aware because they have their own *Commander's Intent* to follow.

Now for you business folks. Simply replace *Commander's Intent* with *Goal* or *Leader's Goal*. You have selected your desired end state, or goal, and told your people what it is. If you are a great leader, you will step out of the way and watch your great women and men strive towards this common goal. Of course, as leaders we must constantly supervise in order to keep things headed in the right direction. However, supervision and controlling are two different things. Supervision will be received well and inspires your people to perform using their own fresh ideas all along the way. Controlling destroys motivation and initiative. It results in bad attitudes toward the goal and the leader. Micromanagement is a type of controlling behavior. I look at micromanagement as interference whereas supervision is ensuring your mission is accomplished in accordance with your *Commander's Intent*. Additionally, a great leader is always available to his people to answer questions and give advice when needed.

You may also refer to your goals as vision. While some of you may think vision can be used to replace *Commander's Intent* as well, I wouldn't recommend it. I say this because vision means something slightly different to me. Vision is more of an overarching, long term view that you, as the leader, have for your organization. Not necessarily the goal that you are attempting to reach in the next week or month, but the direction you are trying to take your company in the next one to five years. Vision is not mission specific but a representation of your present and future plans for your organization.

Lessons Learned

- Great leaders show their people how to think, not what to think.

- Leaders who micromanage and control their people will destroy motivation and initiative, both key ingredients to a successful organization.
- Supervision is necessary to ensure mission accomplishment according to your Commander's Intent.

CHAPTER 25
ATTAINABLE GOALS - ADJUSTABLE GOALS

Set realistic goals and adjust as needed

In all actuality, this makes no sense. Why would you set realistic goals and change them midstream? Well, as leaders, that is exactly what we are charged to do. Is your goal mission accomplishment? If it is, the goal cannot change. Or can it?

You have a mission. As a military leader, the definition of a mission may have a slightly different twist than the business executive's mission statement. As a military leader, this mission could be a combat mission or a somewhat more benign, yet still important, mission. As you move your unit towards the accomplishment of this mission, roadblocks or changing situations may cause a change. Being hard-set on sticking with the original plan, regardless of changing circumstances, could actually cause you to fail. Therefore, analyzing the task at hand and deciding if the risk outweighs the reward is an important leadership trait to possess. Don't get me wrong, there is always risk. We cannot be risk averse. I say again, we cannot be risk averse. But we must understand the consequences of ignoring imminent risk simply because we have set an unchangeable goal.

I have seen leaders who have been clearly shown that failure will be the outcome of the task at hand if they do not deviate from their original plan. Yet, even with indisputable proof of imminent failure, they are compelled to stick to their previous goal or plan. A truly great leader will show his or her inner confidence by simply stopping the madness before it gets out of their control.

> A mission was handed to our key leaders in Iraq. We were tasked to enter an area of Fallujah which was the hiding place of a key terrorist leader. As the mission planning began, we quickly realized we were headed into a hornets' nest. This area was in complete control of the terrorists. There was not a structure in sight of the targeted building which could be trusted. Any Americans who had entered this area in the past had been engaged violently by the local inhabitants. So this question was asked: Is this man important enough to get a number of operators killed in the process of his capture? The undisputed answer was "No." This man was considered important, but intelligence did not feel his capture would lead us to any leaders higher up the food chain.
>
> The men who were planning this mission quickly decided the time was not right for the mission at hand. There would be another time and place to capture this individual. The risk outweighed the importance of the raid. After this discussion, the Commander was approached and given a quick synopsis of the decision making process we followed to come to the aborting of this mission. He did not like the fact we were changing the plan mid-stroke. He did not want to hear this mission was "not smart" even if that message was coming from the men who were to be the ones on the ground executing it. He and his executive officer were not going to let this mission be stopped. It was

going to happen, regardless of the risks. To this day, I will never understand why. There was no significant tactical or strategic reason for the mission. Once we were told the mission would be a go no matter our reasoning, we put our heads together in order to limit the number of casualties as best we could. We would go in extremely heavily armed and ensure that our Rules of Engagement were followed to the letter of the law. All threats would be eliminated. We would not allow the terrorists in the area to gain an advantage. We would be as aggressive as possible.

As luck would have it, we had a great combat proven leader at a higher level within the chain of command that got wind of this poorly picked mission. He wondered why we would even attempt entering this area until the battlefield had changed in our favor. He immediately applied the brakes in order to stop what could have been a possible suicide mission. This leader had nothing to prove. His thought process was directed towards ensuring that goals were attainable and, at this point, the mission's success was questionable. Therefore, he aborted the mission. In doing so, he once again, proved himself as a great combat leader.

Why would the first leader not change the plan when intelligence told him it would be suicidal? A mere guess would be he did not want to lose face in front of his executive officer or the other officers appointed below him. To this day, I still don't quite understand his thought process. The important lesson is there was a crew of good leaders who were making the right decisions; they were passing along the importance of researching the reason and need for this mission in the first place. If all of the leaders involved had been in lockstep with one another and scared to adjust the goal as needed; the outcome might have been a catastrophic failure.

If the situation changes, then change the situation

Situations change all the time in business and on the battlefield. You don't know exactly who your customer will be tomorrow. In business, your customers change due to markets and advertising. In the military, your customers change because they are a new or adapting enemy. Where will the next threat come from in regard to business or military operations? In law enforcement, suspects are looking for innovative ways to outsmart cops. If you, as a leader, are not changing as the situation changes, you will never be successful. In military operations, the threat is looking for a better way to outsmart your soldiers. If you don't stay ahead of that threat, you and your people's lives are in serious peril.

In business, threat equals competitive businesses that are looking to outsmart, out innovate, or out-earn your company. They may simply just want to take a market share away from your business. If you don't stay ahead in business, your livelihood is in jeopardy; this doesn't just affect the CEO, this causes detriment to each and every member of your team.

During combat operations many commanders felt "presence patrols" somehow helped with their overall mission success. "Presence patrols" simply means convoys or soldiers would patrol through a predetermined area to show a presence. For the terrorists, this presented a perfect target for their roadside bombings and sniper operations. Many soldiers were killed or maimed during these presence patrols. Commanders lost sight of the fact that the

situation had changed. If they had chosen to change the situation and only patrolled towards a known objective, many lives could have been saved. Being disciplined enough to not establish a pattern can only help our friendly forces avoid planned traps.

As they say, "hindsight is 20/20." Many brave men and women conducted these presence patrols daily. It is unfortunate that military leaders at all levels continued to allow this to happen. Nothing was gained and there was everything to lose simply because leaders were not willing to *"Set realistic goals and adjust as needed."* The *situation had changed,* but leaders chose not to *change the situation.*

Lessons Learned

- If the situation changes, then change the situation.
- Continuous re-evaluation of goals throughout the planning and execution phases of the mission while operating within a dynamic or changing environment is critical to mission success.

CHAPTER 26
AVOIDING BUREAUCRACY

Bureaucracy: A system of administration marked by officialism, red tape and proliferation.[1]

What can I say if you are part of a bureaucratic organization? You are doomed to a life of red tape just as the definition above says. There are people in England who have the title "bureaucrat," which truly means an unelected official. Regardless, condemnation to a life of torturous chasing of your tail is not a good thing. Bureaucrat can also mean those who sit at a desk.

The American meaning of bureaucracy, at least to a military man, is that of stubborn stupidity which does not allow for a smooth system of problem solving. Additionally, it can describe the many roadblocks erected in the path of those striving towards mission accomplishment and success.

Organizations need checks and balances to ensure they are not going rogue and destroying people's rights, wrecking their savings accounts, or maybe even going to jail. We must supervise to keep people on azimuth. There is a huge difference between these necessary checks and balances and bureaucracy. Bureaucracy will stifle initiative and eventually bankrupt motivation.

Some leaders feel adding bureaucracy will enable them to better manage their people. Keep them busy with paperwork and they will be more manageable. This is probably a true statement; they will be more manageable because they will not have any motivation left. Lack of motivation will lead to lack of initiative; lack of initiative will lead to lack of results. Lack of results is a term I call *failure*. Failure is not where we want to be. If we fail after giving 110 percent, then we can learn from that. If we fail because we never really got going due to roadblocks in our path, we have even more to learn.

Shield your people from bureaucracy

Many leaders I talk to are really fed up with the rules and regulations they must follow; rules which are not helping them attain mission completion and do nothing to maintain good order. Many rules have been put in place to stop what some leaders perceive as trouble before it starts. Or you may have rules in place to slow down productive people enough for the leader to catch up. If this is the case, you need more nimble leaders and less red tape. Let those producers run.

If you are the leader who has had enough, stop the madness. You are now in the position to change the way things are done in your organization. Just because bureaucracy was accepted by previous leaders doesn't mean you have to follow suit. Take a stand and be worthy. Your people deserve to be productive. It is your job to shield them from bureaucracy. Be worthy of your leadership position by holding up your end of the bargain and doing everything in your power to serve and protect your people when justified.

CHAPTER 26 AVOIDING BUREAUCRACY

From a Special Forces Team Sergeant:

> *This is the EXACT reason why we have Special Forces Detachment Commanders. A good Detachment Commander will provide TOP COVER for the detachment while the Team Sergeant conducts operations, training, and day-to-day activities. They (18A Special Forces Officer) are on the team to learn and be mentored by the 18Z (Special Forces Team Sergeant) and to provide that TOP COVER, acting as a liaison between the team and command (Company and Battalion). The amount of bureaucracy in which we must endure to train and operate these days is painful. The Detachment Commander needs to sift through it, block, and or deflect it so that the 18Z (Team Sergeant) and the rest of detachment can train and focus on mission accomplishment.*

In the military and LE community, it is extremely important that the time from flash to bang is quick. If you don't have a quick response, several things can happen: People will die, officers will be injured, and the suspect will get a chance to repeat his crimes; all of which can have serious consequences. In this day and age, manpower is an issue too. More time wasted means the loss of money or the loss of the ability to accomplish several missions instead of just a single unproductive escapade. Don't get me wrong. There are times we must slow down and be very deliberate about our decision-making. But there are other times we need to get to the important issues and solve the problem.

> *We had a commander who was not very sure of himself or our team. The men in our Unit also didn't trust him or his decision-making capabilities. During our mission planning process he required us to use the*

Military Decision Making Process (MDMP). This process was developed for large unit mission planning at the highest levels. The process allowed commanders to slowly work through problems over several days, or sometimes weeks, to come to a final conclusion of the overall scheme of maneuver. This process requires the planners to come up with three courses of action, evaluate each course of action and, once this is finalized, put the pieces together to form a plan that can be executed on the battlefield. As you might guess, this process is severally limiting to those who are planning for a personnel recovery or time sensitive target which needs attention immediately. So, we continued to do as we were told by our commander. MDMP was employed and we were slow and, quite honestly, the attitudes we developed were not good. The men in our outfit didn't want anything to do with the planning process. They were eventually pushed to the point where they wanted to sit around, wait until the commander made a decision about the plan, and then simply execute his plan. If you haven't figured this out yet, Special Forces soldiers don't do well in a lockstep environment. They are selected for their ability to think outside of the box.

Lockstep: A standard method or procedure that is mindlessly adhered to or that minimizes individuality.[2]

Eventually this commander was replaced by a very competent and confident leader. The men loved him and had the utmost respect for him. He was fair but stern, loud but not obnoxious, smart but not condescending. The first thing he did when he took charge was to sit us down and tell everyone to take

MDMP and throw it out the window. We needed to have bottom up planning. The lowest men on the totem pole would be involved in the process since they would be the individuals entering the breach. Not only would these men be involved with the planning but, by having more people involved in the problem solving process, we would actually develop more than three courses of action as we went and thereby work through which action would get the job done most efficiently. Motivation hit an all-time high. We were much better at not only the planning process, but when the mission was conducted we knew the plan because it was our plan, not the commander's plan. However, as always, he maintained overall approval and responsibility for the plan.

A leader is going to have to make active decisions and not default to the status-quo or take a pass on the hard decisions because he can't make it through red-tape and bureaucracy. If something or someone is holding back progress, the good leader will make every effort to change that system. Not rebuff or ignore it, but actually go about getting it changed for the better. Each person's input is valuable. You want the whole team working together on the Mission Planning Process, but in the end there is a reason the leader is in the "position" that he or she is in. The leader must be ready to make the final decision and lead.

Efficient targets require efficient planning and execution

As leaders we must strive to keep things efficient. Our enemies are efficient. They are constantly looking for better ways to attack us or commit crimes. In business, our competitors are looking for ways to beat us to market. We must let our people get out there and do what they do best to beat our opponents to the punch. Remember, supervising is one thing. Crushing the spirit and initiative of your people with the sledgehammer of bureaucracy is another.

You have great people working for you. They want to make you successful. All you have to do is let them.

Lessons Learned

- Bureaucracy is the enemy of innovation and efficiency.
- Leaders should run interference to keep the bureaucracy at bay and allow their people the freedom to accomplish the mission.

FUTURE LEADERS

CHAPTER 27
SELECTING LEADERS

Two Motor Officers from a large Police Department were gunned down in the streets of America. Later in the day, two SWAT Team Members from the same department were also killed while trying to apprehend the suspect.

This department's SWAT leadership is a perfect example of the results of a poor selection technique. Leaders were selected for political reasons, at least at the lieutenant level. Then this mission comes along; a mission that required leaders who can think on their feet regardless of the mayhem that is going on around them. As the stress level built, these leaders fell apart. They were not even able to follow through on basic Standard Operating Procedures (SOP's) for their organization. From the Chief down, they failed. For LE officers to hold these positions but lack the prerequisite leadership training and crisis management skills is unforgivable. These men should have never been put into these positions. They were not qualified to be a sergeant on the SWAT Team so why would their organization make them lieutenants on the same SWAT Team? Poor decisions were made. Not just the day of this assault, but years prior as well. Specifically, a failed leadership selection and training process caused the needless deaths of two SWAT Team members.

I have had the honor to work with sergeants and officers of this SWAT Team. They are great warriors who understand their mission and train hard to be ready for the next crisis situation no matter what crazy twists the situation may take. I have also had contact with the lieutenants and assistant chiefs. They, on the other hand, appear to be selected for political reasons. These supposed leaders put mission focus, as well as Leadership/Crisis Management training, very low on their scale of importance.

What does your organization need?

You need strong leaders that will take your organization to the next level. You must accomplish your mission. Who is ready to get this done? What qualities do they need to possess?

You need self-motivated individuals who are working even when you are not watching. These self-motivated individuals will be putting in the time needed to elevate your organization even though they are not in a higher position of authority or responsibility. Be honest with yourself and those in your organization when you make these selections. If you truly pick the right man or woman for the right job, you will not regret it.

Past Performance Counts

Who would make a better leader? A former military officer with several combat tours in leadership positions or a college graduate with no previous leadership experience? Of course, we all pick the Army officer. Sure, makes sense. However, several federal law enforcement organizations see this differently. Pay scales and selection for positions are based solely on academic education and not real world leadership education. Even real world education, or as we Army guys call it, *having a job*, is not taken into consideration. In the military, you must perform in your current leadership position before even being considered for an elevated leadership position. Is this always successful? Absolutely not. However, it does let you gauge someone's performance in their current position to see if there is *potential* for them to become a leader at a higher level.

How do we evaluate someone for the next position?

Evaluate individuals with *snapshots in time* from their previous positions. If this doesn't give you enough to work with, you may need to give them a chance to lead. One way to do this is to delegate authority to your subordinates to see how they perform. Just remember, delegating authority does not release you from the overall responsibility for their actions or inaction. Once you delegate, you will see who truly rises to the occasion and proves to you that they are ready for a shot at the next level.

Honesty is the best policy

If you are honest with the folks you work with every day, the selections you make will not come as a surprise. If you plan on going down in history as a Great Leader, you should make all of your subordinates well aware of how you roll. Your subordinates shouldn't be surprised when you pick the best man or woman for the job. This should be your daily Modus Operandi (MO). Show your people that you have a laser lock on the mission at hand. What are the tasks that will make us and our team successful? Who are the people that can get us to our goal by leading our team? These are the individuals we should choose for elevated responsibility. Those that don't see this are not team players.

Why are you in this position?

Often we see individuals who are placed in positions so they can say they were in that position even though they have no reason, idea, or purpose for being there. This is an insult to the productive people in your organization. They all see it. You must select individuals who can move on to higher positions of responsibility when the time comes. However, they must first prove they can perform at the lower level before being promoted to elevated levels.

What is your organization's selection process for being a leader?

Is there a list of standards that must be met? Is there a prerequisite skill set or training that is mandatory for selection to higher levels of responsibility or elevated leadership positions? The sad state of affairs in the world we live is this: Sometimes tenure or time on the job gets in the way of performance and mission focus.

The use of tenure, by itself, is a great example of failed leadership. If your organization uses tenure as the sole source of selection for elevated positions, I can guarantee you and your organization are in a bad way. How can I be so bold as to say this? Well, this isn't my first rodeo.

As the national news has covered for years, tenured teachers are destroying our children's education. The facts presented on that topic paint a bleak, but accurate, picture of a failed public school system. Businesses that elevate poor performers who just happen to be the last man standing, or military and LE organizations that pick the old dog, have witnessed failure time and time again when using this selection technique as criteria for advancement. If you have tenure and are qualified to take the new position, then God bless you. If not, there is a problem with your organization.

How dare I…

If you feel you are being attacked because of the statement that tenure doesn't work I only ask that you take a long hard look at yourself and your organization. Be honest. Are the right people in the right positions to propel your department to the next level?

Checking the box

You have a friend who works for you and he or she is up for a promotion or transfer. They are not qualified for the position, but you place them there anyway. You want this person to get the box checked so they can move on to an even higher position or, maybe, just a better paying one.

Don't do it.

If you want someone to move into a managerial position and they are good at it, then move them. But don't make them flounder in a leadership position just to check a box for advancement. This is a huge mistake and can have massive repercussions in your organization. What is the message you are trying to send? That individual ladder climbing is more important than the organization itself? How will that message resonate when it comes time for members to make sacrifices to accomplish the mission?

Establish your Selection Criteria

If you can develop criteria for leaders in your organization, the selection process will become much easier. A simple checklist of what is needed in a leader will help with this process (Refer to *Chapter 36: Checklists*). Maybe it isn't just what is needed in an individual. Maybe it is also the training, experience, or education which he or she must complete before being eligible for the position; if not before the selection process for increased levels of responsibility, then immediately after it. The bottom line is this: If you are responsible for selecting your subordinate leaders, have a plan. Study that plan, deviate as necessary according to what happens in the real world, but have a plan.

Ranger Leadership Selection

Ranger leaders are required to attend a selection course. This course is called Ranger Orientation Program (ROP). Potential leaders are instructed and evaluated on their skill sets as well as being made aware of the Ranger Regiment's Standard Operating Procedures (SOP) which they would be required to follow. If a potential leader fails this program, he is sent back to the Regular Army. At least, that is the standard. Pre-Mogadishu, one particular Ranger leader, the battalion commander, did not successfully complete ROP but he was still allowed to become the battalion commander. Did this have consequences in Mogadishu? I know what the Rangers think. They have no doubt his failures added to the complexity of that fateful day in Mogadishu. But ultimately it was the regimental commander who failed his men by putting an unqualified person into a leadership position. The battalion commander's unacceptable performance was simply the manifestation of that failure.

Every Ranger knew of their commander's ROP failure and that doesn't help your morale as a young Ranger, enlisted or commissioned.

Since the good old days of the early 90's, Ranger Selection has changed. It is currently called Ranger Assessment and Selection Program (RASP). It is an 8-week course held at Fort Benning, Georgia. RASP is required for all Ranger ranks. As of 2010, RASP replaced both Ranger Indoctrination Program (RIP) for enlisted personnel, and the Ranger Orientation Program (ROP) for Officers and Non-Commissioned Officers. Every soldier or officer assigned to the U.S. Army's 75th Ranger Regiment must attend and pass the course for inclusion into the Regiment. To put this in perspective for the civilian side of society, ROP, or RASP, is the equivalent of an entry-level prerequisite college course but with a lot more physical training and a lot less sleep and food.

Lessons Learned

- What are your criteria for being a leader?
- Past experience and past performance should be the determining factor for leadership selection.
- Establish a list of the criteria for potential future leaders to meet.
- Give your people elevated responsibilities and see how they perform.

CHAPTER 28
WHAT IS YOUR PROMOTION PROCESS?

So whom should you choose to lead your team? Do we promote from within or seek help from outside? What process do you follow to get the right people into leadership positions?

Leadership selection and the promotion process are really two different things but training is the key element in both. As you provide realistic leadership training to all of your people, you will see how it shakes out and select those who deserve further training.

Training equals education and experience equals education. Therefore, when I use the term training you can simply replace this with education. As we train, we are receiving our education, which will be used as a defining element of the selection and promotion process. From those selectees, or trainees, you will determine who actually gets the promotion. As the trainees move along this path, you must watch to see who is performing. Performance is key to selecting those for promotion.

Written Testing

What is your promotion process? Is it simply a written test that applicants take and see how they do? This is the case in many law enforcement organizations as well as the United States Air Force. A written test evaluation can help with the promotion process but it should not be the only tool you use to select your leaders. In many jurisdictions, a written exam process, along with lack of experience-based promotions, have stifled the ability of a unit or team to be successful. Good test takers who lack experience rarely make good leaders. This system also discourages certain others from putting their hats into the ring. Police officers and Air Force operators who really like their job and work hard to perform their daily duties often fail miserably on written tests. Real world experience is on their side, but they will never make it past the written test gate to be considered for promotion.

> *The perfect example is the US Air Force Combat Control Team (CCT) Operators. These boys are combat forces who specialize in air traffic control and fire support from fast movers (jet fighters) as well as attack helicopters. They also provide command and control functions through unlimited communication capabilities. Their motto is "First there" and it is the truth. No matter the composition of a group of Army or Navy Special Operators on the battlefield, an Air Force CCT is always there. These warriors are the irreplaceable men that operate in any environment. They are great at parachuting, whether it is static line or free fall. They are SCUBA qualified, so waterborne missions are not an issue. They are also great marksmen and physically fit. These men are constantly deployed worldwide. Their schedule doesn't allow them time to get in the needed studying to pass a promotional test. I served on the battlefield with many of these warriors and their skills are irreplaceable. Yet, they were not being promoted. Can't pass the test, can't get promoted. Passing would be a simple matter for them if they were allowed to test on the gear and techniques they use on a daily*

basis in combat environments. However, the testing is academic and has no application to the real world in which they live.

Some will say that those operators, or law officers, who want to do well need to simply study and take the test along with the others who lack real world experience. Not so fast. That first group of men and women are really busy accomplishing their mission. They are accountable to those around them. They understand that if they don't do their jobs to the best of their ability each and every day, others will suffer... or worse. So, am I saying that those who do well on the test have been half-stepping? No, not in all cases, this is just another standard of measure. But many times the wrong folks end up passing this important gate and get one step closer to promotion.

If you choose to incorporate a written exam into your promotion process, make it a realistic test that allows superiors to determine what man or woman they want leading their people. The test must be based on real world job skills that will be used every day, not some arbitrary academic standard.

Experience Counts

Organizations which require experience for promotion are way ahead of those which don't. Some might call this tenure but I prefer to call it getting the experiences needed for promotion under your belt. Merely serving time in a position, or tenure, doesn't count. Time performing is what counts. In the US Army, you must have documented leadership experience in your current pay grade, and not just for a few months, but for an extended period of time. In fact, you will get promoted even quicker if you have experience in the next higher pay grade; real world experience. This method is not always a failsafe which guarantees the right people get into the right positions, but it is pretty reliable. When I see the problems the test takers cause when they are put into leadership roles, I can easily say that experience is king.

Promoting from Within

> One man and his E-commerce team are responsible for producing 10 percent of a business's revenue. This individual is overlooked for promotion time after time. He doesn't even get an office while others, with much lower productivity, are being promoted and offered additional shares in the company. In fact, not only doesn't he get promoted, he doesn't even get reimbursed for his moving expenses, and the company won't even put his name on their organizational chart. When asked, he says he doesn't feel he is appreciated. How can a business overlook someone who has proven himself a leader by having an E-commerce team that, time and again, crushes projections? Finally, reluctantly, he takes an offer from another company. Now his original company wants to know why? If he was up to the task, why wasn't he selected? If he wasn't up to the task, why wasn't he counseled? If you choose not to reward or promote proven leaders from within, there will always be another organization that will happily swoop in and take them off your hands. This is great for the man or woman you have passed over and great for their new employer. That may have not been your intent, but you are still accountable for what happened.

Promoting from within makes sense. Or does it? It seems some CEOs always want to hire from outside of their organizations and never promote the talent inside their own castle walls. I wholeheartedly disagree with this practice. If you already have the talent within your organization and they are ready to step up to the next level, let them. It is discouraging to the loyal individuals in your organization when they see there is no way in Hades they will get promoted to the next level of leadership or even a managerial position. Low morale will follow. If you are a leader who wants your people to look at you as credible, actions like this will ensure that never happens. Why would they see you as credible when you are not using the talent you have right under your nose? Promoting from within inspires loyalty and longevity if you have the right people ready for elevated levels of responsibility.

But what if? What if you don't have the talent in house or your organization's leadership development has grown stale? Then it is extremely important to get someone from outside to come in and get the boat headed in the right direction. Outside hires may be the breath of fresh air which is needed. This is depressing for the people who feel they have been faithful. But, if you want success, and they aren't performing at the needed level, this is the way it has to be. How do you deal with someone who feels they have been ignored? How do you hire from outside and overlook this faithful follower that you know hasn't the ability to move up? How about you man up and tell them to their face. If you have subordinates that are not up to the task, they should already know. If you have honestly counseled them, it won't come as a surprise. If you are scared to talk with them, it might just be time to grow up. If these poor performers lose what little motivation they have, you will have to be accountable for that. This is why you are the leader. We never said it was going to be easy.

Tenure

As I have said in the past, and I will say again, promoting based solely on tenure does not work. Period. Over and over again we have witnessed tenure destroy schools and organizations by only promoting the longest lasting employees. Simply being a survivor in your organization doesn't set you up for success. If you are the most qualified, and have the longevity to go along with it, great, you should be promoted. You, as a leader, must look around and decide who truly deserves to be elevated in your organization: The producers or the entitled?

Lessons Learned

- Written tests, by themselves, are insufficient to justify promotion.
- Look for future leaders inside your organization before going outside.
- Tenure is not a surefire step up the ladder.

CHAPTER 29
TRAINING LEADERS

Since retiring from active military duty, I have run many Mission Planning Courses. These courses involve tasking leaders to do the following: receiving the mission, briefing the mission plan, supervising the rehearsal of the mission, making key decisions during the conduct of the mission, and, in the end, critiquing not only the members of their team but taking a long hard look at their own performance. During one such course, we had a group of young men from Air Force Special Operations attend. Many of the law enforcement men and women in attendance were, at first, tentative of these young warriors. They were young, they were full of spunk, they talked a lot of trash, and they were not experienced law enforcement professionals to which these officers were accustomed. However, once we started the planning process and the mission briefs, there was a whole new side to these Air Force operators. They briefed extremely well, they were confident, they worked well as a team, and they ALL had mission focus for the task at hand as well as for their daily Air Force mission. Many of the police in attendance pulled me to the side to say how proud they were of these fellas when put into a performance position. This high performance was not in any way due to the course I was teaching at the time but was a direct reflection on their past training/education. They had been briefing their peers as well as others outside of their community for several years. There were a few combat veterans in their midst which helped add real world focus. They had leaders who tried their best to shield their men from bureaucracy so they could focus on the mission and the training which was required to be a savvy special operations airman. The bottom line was this: they had been trained to lead.

Some leadership gurus would lead you to believe that leaders are born. Ok, stop right there. Unless you are born to a king and queen, you are not born a leader. Sorry, I call them like I see them. So let's say you are born a leader in England, does this mean you will be a great leader? More than likely not. However, if you get the correct mentoring as a child, followed up with the proper leadership training, you may become that very rare animal, a born leader. Of course, there are an awful lot of steps in the right direction you must take to make this truly happen. However if, like me, you are one of those whose family fled England and Sweden (or any other country for that matter) for the chance to build a great nation, you might want to think about what training or education is needed to become a leader.

Leadership training is something that is often overlooked in business and law enforcement. Individuals believe they are ready to lead simply because they took a test (LE) or because they have been selected by someone above their pay grade (business). Both examples will often put the wrong person in the job and that can have dire effects on your business or your mission.

> *In the Selecting Leaders Chapter we mentioned officers and civilians who were put in charge of their city's police force and SWAT Team. The scary thing is those in charge didn't, and still don't, have the training they need to handle a crisis such as the one we discussed in the Selecting Leaders chapter. There are required, common sense guidelines that*

CHAPTER 29 TRAINING LEADERS

are supposed to be followed when events like those we discussed unfolded. They are there to ensure that everyone is on the same sheet of music and for leaders, as well as individual officers, to be brought up to date on all of the specifics of the mission. During a crisis situation there are rules on the tactical side of the house that we must follow. One of these is to establish a Tactical Command Post (TCP) in order to have a centralized location for Tactical Officers to be briefed and to gather the intelligence needed to make sound decisions in the tactical environment. In this situation, the TCP was never established. Another fact, often overlooked, is that there was never an Incident Command Post (ICP) established either. The establishment of an ICP is a prerequisite to the establishment of a TCP according to this Police Department's policy.

The Independent Board of Inquiry (BOI) into this event, which came out in December 2009, states the following:

> Board of Inquiry Finding- Absent exigent circumstances, there was no urgency to order an expedited entry into the apartment. The BOI found that the order to force entry was not in compliance with the PD Policies and practices.
>
> Board of Inquiry Recommendations- PD should consider re-training supervisors, command staff, and executive staff in sound tactical principles. Deficient practices should be identified and corrected to reflect policy requirements and best practices.

On this day, the Incident Commander and the Tactical Commander were extremely negligent in their duties. But if we look deeper into the situation, the true blame for the poor decisions made falls squarely on the shoulders of <u>their</u> leaders. The commanders were selected even though they lacked the wherewithal to handle a crisis like the one looking them directly in the face that day. At the very least, they should have been expected to follow the policies of their Police Department and the Incident Command System. However, they failed to do any of this because they were never trained to do otherwise.

I have traveled to this area many times to train state officers as well as individuals from their Team. To date, I have not had a single member of this Police Department's leadership attend training. This is a sad state of affairs for this group of SWAT men and women. Their leaders simply feel that merely being in an elevated position gives them the knowledge to make the correct decisions when a crisis erupts.

As I have said many times, this team is ready. They know how to operate and they can handle a dynamic situation. It is their leaders who I have found to be lacking the requisite training and experience to deal with a crisis.

You as a leader must give your people the training they need.

Are your people lacking leadership training? If they are, you must be held accountable. Leadership training is much harder to administer than your normal day-to-day training. While basic firearms and equal opportunity training are very important, they are much easier blocks of instruction to present than leadership training. Leadership training may involve scenarios and, more than likely, bringing in outsiders who have the skill set to train your leaders at this level. Additionally, leadership training requires leaders to take the time to improve their capabilities. Finally, this training requires the leaders' superiors to fully support their people while they strive for this improvement.

Leadership is a difficult skill that must be taught and trained.

Once your leaders (or you for that matter) have been selected for training, you must slow down and give them the tools they need. You can't throw them in the deep end of the pool and hope they swim. Well, you can, but it won't work. You have to allow them the time to be taught the decision-making and people leading skills they will need to be successful.

As you teach subordinate leaders to hopefully, one day, take your place; remember what it was like when you were new to that position. Were you able to think clearly at all times and always make the perfect decision? More than likely not. You should remember what it was like to learn from your training.

They will make mistakes. When a mistake is made in training, we learn more from it than if everything went perfectly. If you are training your people and they never fail, you are accomplishing nothing. Failure is a great facilitator to learning.

We must train these leaders "how to think" not "what to think."

The situations you and I have been in are completely different. The situations your people will get into are also different from what you have experienced. You can't always fight the last war; you must look ahead and be prepared for the next war. If you are taught to utilize only one way of linear thinking, you will be in rough shape. If you are taught to deal with an ever-changing problem, contingencies won't be a challenge. Give your people the tools to think through the problem and find their solution. Not your solution, theirs… More than likely it will be different. It may not be to your liking, but will it get all of you to the same mission accomplishment at the end of the day? If so, great, have them drive on. If not, stop the process, have them learn from it, and continue to the team's overarching goal.

If you have selected someone to groom for a leadership position, don't let their training be at the expense of your group's performers or those who are already developed enough to take that position. These performers can become stagnant and lose their motivation if they are not put to good use as members of the team. Also, make sure your organization and the mission doesn't suffer because of whom you have selected to groom for the leadership position. I have seen this happen a few times in the military. You have many individuals who are extremely qualified to take a position but, for whatever reason, you decide that you want someone else instead. At the end of the day, if you simply pick the right person for the job (the performer, the qualified individual) mission accomplishment, along with team building, will go much smoother. Look way down the road for your organization, not just to the first speed bump.

Let Them Learn

Once you make the call on leader selection, let them jump in the pool. I can't emphasis enough that you have to let them make a few mistakes so they can learn. This is accomplished in the training phase, not after they are moved into the elevated position of responsibility. Let them venture into the deep end of the pool on their own and see how they do. As a mentor, you should be proud to see your people get out and learn from experience. Hopefully, there will come a day when they surpass you. This is the highest form of mentorship.

Leadership Checklists

When you get on an airplane does the pilot use a checklist? I hope so. If not, you might want to hurry up and get out while you can. Leadership is the same. You, as a leader, must use a checklist to help you make decisions quickly. For some, this checklist isn't something they pull out of their pocket. It is in their head. As a new leader, don't be afraid to use a checklist to help you efficiently get through the planning or decision making process. In the military, we use checklists for everything and at the end of the day it helps to keep us efficient during times of stress or exhaustion. These lists also are great training aides for your junior leaders.

Here is a simple list that I have used for years:

Troop Leading Procedures
- ❏ Receive the Mission
- ❏ Issue the Warning Order
- ❏ Make Tentative Plan
- ❏ Initiate Movement
- ❏ Conduct Recon
- ❏ Complete the Plan
- ❏ Issue the Order
- ❏ Supervise/Rehearse

Doesn't seem like a very in-depth checklist? But this list will help you get through those tough situations. Each point on this list has a series of instructions we will need to follow to get the task completed. Bottom line: Don't be afraid of checklists, they really work.

Lessons Learned

- Leadership is a skill that is learned, not a trait with which one is born.
- Give your future leaders a task and let them learn on their own while you supervise.
- Failure is a great facilitator to learning.

CHAPTER 30
SELECTING SUBORDINATES

If you, as a leader, are ever fortunate enough to select your own subordinates, you are sitting on the top of the world. You have the ability to set your team up for complete success. Or, if you don't make the right selections, you may be steadily moving your organization towards failure.

So when the time comes, how will you determine who will come onboard to work with you? Will you look at the past positions which an individual has held and determine if they have checked all of the boxes to be in this new position? If so, you may have just failed the test of team building. Selecting individuals who are position oriented rather than performance focused is, and always will be, a problem. Many times I have seen selectees for business leadership or subordinate leadership slots evaluated entirely on their past list of positions, i.e. their résumé. Performance was second on the list during the evaluation. Taking a position for the sole purpose of using it as a stepping-stone to elevated titles or increased pay levels is not an indicator of future success. You should be taking this position for elevated levels of responsibility and the yearning to lead people, make a difference, and complete the mission.

If you are looking at a candidate's past performance, in spite of the positions they held, you will be on the right track. I define a candidate's past performance as tasks completed, successful missions, and their organization's well-being after they departed. As you select individuals based on performance, you will have those who can be mentored to someday fill leadership positions in your organization. The opposite is not true. If you hire strictly based on prior position and it doesn't work, you are stuck. At the very least, you will have to go through the termination process to get rid of your mistake. If you pigeon hole yourself by bringing a big position guy on board, you may get just that: A big talker with an extensive Rolodex who hasn't performed on his or her own in years. Merely occupying a position has nothing to do with performance. On the opposite side of the equation, if you hire strictly based on performance, you have choices. If the individual fails to perform, you will still be forced to remove or replace him. This process will not be an easy one. However, if their record shows solid performance you, as the leader, should be able to cultivate their past performance and increase their capacity in their new setting. If you have a great performer who can be placed in elevated positions of responsibility it is a simple matter of changing their title.

Do you want people that require spurs or brakes?

Have you ever thought about running into a burning building? I have and it isn't high on my priority list. It is definitely not going to make any bucket list, even if I had such a thing. So what in the world is wrong with firemen? They choose to run into buildings that are on fire. How odd is that? But aren't you glad there are men and women who do this? I know I am. So what would firefighting be like if these individuals required spurs rather than brakes? There would be a Fire Chief pushing people towards the burning building trying to convince them to go inside. Not a recipe for success. I am one of those who would need that type of coaxing to enter a burning building. Now, if you told me there was a terrorist inside who I could eliminate, I am all in.

CHAPTER 30 SELECTING SUBORDINATES

It doesn't take long to decide you want folks working for you who are self-starters; motivated in spite of the circumstances at hand. Many leaders want people working for them who give 110%, but only when the leader sees fit. Well, this isn't the way it works. Most individuals who give 110% are always on. This being said, don't be surprised if the performer gets into a little mischief when they are off duty as well. Remember, they are the ones who give 110% whether at work or play.

As a Sergeant Major, I was reviewing records for a promotion board to Sergeant First Class. I had been selected to represent the Special Operations community as a promotion board member, an honor and quite a chore I would find out later. We were tasked with developing the standards by which the applicants would be rated. Once the standards were set we began reviewing records to see who would make the cut according to our standards. I had an impeccable record come across my desk. This young Ranger had numerous trips overseas in support of the Global War on Terror. He had a spotless performance evaluation and many citations for bravery and extreme performance in equally extreme conditions. He had proven himself worthy of a promotion by filling elevated positions of responsibility and performing all along the way. There was one small glitch. After an extended deployment, he had returned to the United States where he was now allowed to drink. He hadn't been able to do this down range. Only the Muslims and the Generals get to partake while in Muslim Lands.

So the young soldier and his friends went out and got a little liquored up. At this point his motivation was still 110 percent, just focused on the wrong thing.

> *He stood on top of someone's Hybrid car and, with the greatest of ease, performed the atomic full body elbow slam. This easily blew out every window of the vehicle. Now you have a great soldier with a spotless military record involved in an alcohol related incident. So... what do you do? I was torn. I knew this individual was a performer; he required brakes not spurs. Now he had out ran his headlights. He had been punished for this transgression and I felt he should still be promoted since he should have already learned his lesson. Oh, and by the way, we are promoting Warriors here, not choirboys.*
>
> *And just in case you are wondering...*
> *we promoted him.*

I suppose I am a little old fashioned. When I first came into the Army, we were given the benefit of the doubt. You were definitely punished for any wrongdoing but your career wasn't ruined because of a little bit of letting off some steam. I do feel there are times subordinates cannot be forgiven. There are lines which must not be crossed. You, as a leader, must determine where you draw that line.

It all comes down to you making the call as to who you select to work for you. But why are you making this selection? If you have certain prerequisite selection criteria which must be met, that is great as long as the right people are being selected. Past performance should be the key ingredient no matter your mission. If you are running a business, it is about the bottom line. So, at the end of the day, all your workers, at all levels, must perform. If you are in the military or law enforcement, it is still about the bottom line: mission accomplishment. We need dedicated performers moved into positions of elevated responsibility if they are a proven fit. Past performance does not guarantee future performance, but it does give you a better chance of success than selecting a proven non-performer. Don't get sucked into fancy titles that look good on paper. What is the bottom line? The bottom line is performance.

Selecting Subordinates Checklist

Here is a list of points I use to evaluate candidates and explanations for each point.

Performance – Has this person performed in the past and will they perform in the future? I am a big fan of qualitative performance over quantitative performance. Qualitative is subjective but it lets me evaluate the person's abilities and skills by my standards.

Potential – What is the realm of possibilities with this individual? In a year or two will they be able to move up the ladder and perform at a higher level or is this person always going to be the #4 man on a 6 man team?

110% – As the earlier story pointed out, if you expect 110% at work then you will more than likely get 110% at play. This is something I want from a performer. Now, I don't want them to spend time in jail, but being a little over the edge is not always bad.

Mission Organization – Can this person determine the flow of an operation without guidance, understand what threats we may encounter, and have a plan to avoid or deal with those threats?

Aggressiveness – In the business I was in, we needed aggression. Being mean and being aggressive are two different things. Bullies are mean, warriors are aggressive. There is similar aggressive behavior in the business world as well.

Confidence –They must be sure of themselves without being over the top cocky. A little cocky and a little confidence are very similar. However, confidence is only good if they have the skills to back it up.

Thinking outside of the box – I want a subordinate who will come up with great ideas which the rest of the team has not thought about. I want someone who will challenge my thinking as well.

Daring – As the British SAS motto says, "He who dares, wins."

Enjoys life, including their job – If you enjoy life and your job you will more than likely be a great fit on my team.

Honest – The candidate must be able to be trusted at all times. In the warfighter business this is a must. In the business world this is a must as well.

Approachable – A subordinate who is aloof is not going to work out. I have had subordinates who thought they were smarter than everyone when in fact they left a lot to be desired. A candidate needs to be down to earth.

Strong core values (Morals and Ethics) – I want someone who stands up for what they believe in and lives by those morals and ethical standards at work and at home.

Can take criticism – I want subordinates who admit when they are wrong, reflect on their failures, and improve. You must have thick skin and be able to handle criticism.

Loyalty – Does loyalty come into consideration for you?

Lessons Learned

- The criteria you set for selecting subordinates will determine the tone of your work place and future success of your mission. Take this seriously.
- Past performance is an excellent predictor of future results.
- Do you want team members who need spurs or brakes?

CHAPTER 31
COMPLIANCE VS. COMMITMENT

Threats + Power + Position = COMPLIANCE

Is this the way you operate? Do you feel that you have to use threats to get things done? How about using your power or position to get results? Of course, there is a time when this may be necessary. If you look back through history, our country has been involved in many wars. During some of these we didn't have a professional Army as we do today. Without professional soldiers and leaders, there will always be some threats and use of power to get folks to comply. This is not the preferred way of doing business but a forceful leader can make things happen when necessary.

Compliance = Adequacy < Greatness

In other words, if people are forced to comply, you as a leader may potentially attain adequate performance from your subordinates; however this adequate performance will always be *less than* greatness.

If you get folks to simply comply, you will merely get the job done. But you will never have the greatness for which you are truly striving. If you are happy with just being adequate, then compliance is for you. Greatness will require a different manner of leadership.

Credibility = Intense Commitment

If you are a credible leader, you will have an *intense commitment* from your subordinates. This *intense commitment* will take you, as a leader, to places you never imagined possible. You will have folks looking out for you, making sure they dot the I's and cross the T's. Once you attain this intense commitment, you will see the success that comes from having a great team which works well together.

> During the US Civil War's Battle of Gettysburg, the Confederate Army sustained huge loses on the third day of the battle. They were forced to attack uphill across an enormous area of open ground into a prepared breastwork in which the Union army had emplaced. On this day, there were definitely **threats** from the Confederate sergeants to get their inadequately trained privates to cross this no man's land. The sergeants had to use their **power and position** to force the soldiers to do their job. Additionally, the soldiers were fighting and dying on that field beside their brothers and uncles. Not only that, it was the 3rd of July, 1863 and they were outfitted in their light weight, quick drying wool uniforms, or not. These uniforms were actually heavy and hot, although by this time in the war many of the men had worn their clothing to tatters. After this fateful attack, later named Picket's Charge, the Confederate soldiers were forced to retreat back to their lines. The front line leaders felt they had failed their overall leader, General Lee. They wanted to get their lines organized and charge again even though the odds for success were not even remotely in their favor. They did this out of admiration for General Lee and couldn't stand the thought they had let him

CHAPTER 31 COMPLIANCE VS. COMMITMENT

down. They knew he was a **credible** leader and they undoubtedly gave him an **intense commitment** even if that meant charging the Union lines once more.

There were successes and failures during the Battle of Gettysburg. General Lee did not know the disposition of the Union Lines. His cavalry commander, J.E.B. Stuart, had decided to gallivant around the countryside instead of gathering the intelligence that his commander needed. Stuart decided, on his own, that raiding some Union supply lines for his own personal glory was more important than conducting the critical, although more mundane, reconnaissance work which would gather the intelligence that his boss, General Lee, badly needed. General Stuart had failed to perform this duty in previous battles. However, time after time, General Lee failed to reprimand his subordinate regarding this matter. So, in this pivotal battle of the Civil War, we see General Lee reap what he had sown due to his failure to lead.[1]

To be successful, you must have committed followers because there is no way to get to your goal on your own. *Intense commitment* by a group of intelligent, hard working men and women is what drives business and the military to success each and every day in America. Great leaders inspire intense commitment; you don't have to be in a great civil war battle to inspire those in your midst. By always being the leader that instills work ethic, fairness, and mission focus, whether for battle or business, your subordinates will gladly provide that *intense commitment*. Be a great leader, get the commitment.

As you lead, you need to decide what you want: adequate performance through compliance or great performance through *intense commitment*.

Great Leader = Intense Commitment

Lessons Learned

- Credible leaders inspire intense commitment from their people.
- Less than credible leaders have to force their people into compliance.

"The power of noble deeds is to be preserved and passed on to the future."

-- Joshua Lawrence Chamberlain

CHAPTER 32
COUNSELING

Large companies, as well as the military and law enforcement, waste plenty of time and hot air on the never-ending leadership discussion. When in fact, all your people really need to know is exactly where you stand. But how can they know what you expect from them if you don't counsel them? Counseling is a tool that should be used frequently rather than sparingly, beginning on the first day they enter your organization. Of course, you can overdo it. If your counseling sessions are merely you telling those who work for you exactly how to complete the task, you're engaged in what we call micromanaging.

Counseling is not the same as discipline or disciplinary actions. Unfortunately, the two have become blurred and often mean the same thing in some organizations. Counseling should be used to guide your people in the direction you desire. Counseling should be looked at as a mentoring tool more than a disciplinary tool. A major part of leadership is to be a coach, a mentor, and a teacher. Use your counseling sessions as an opportunity to be those things to your people.

Initial Counseling

The first chance you have to sit and talk with a new member of your team is the first chance you have to instill your goals and mission focus on this clean slate. This is also a good time to figure out what makes this person tick when they aren't at work. How many kids? How many wives? Hopefully the second one isn't a high number. What do they do for fun? Where did they grow up? What are their goals?

You have this chance to make a first impression and receive one as well. You are in charge at this point so you may not get the full answers, but you should be able to figure out what is inside of this new member of your team.

Get to know the person. Then let them get to know you and your goals as well. They need to know what your definition of success is for your organization and for an individual who works for you. This could be the *Commander's Intent* or a job performance review. They need to know what is expected of them as well as your right and left limits.

What do you want to hear?

When you go into a counseling session with one of your bosses, what do you want to hear? When I ask this question I normally hear, "I want to hear I am doing great." Ok, this is fine if you are truly doing great but, I must say, you will be much better off in the long run if your boss starts with some positives and then quickly moves on to some constructive criticism. This is counseling, not discipline.

Good or bad, be honest

When it comes right down to it, after just a little introspection, most of you want to be great. You want to know how to improve. Give your people the same benefit of the doubt. You should look at each man or woman who steps in front of you as someone who wants to be the absolute best they can be. The only way you can help them during this counseling session is to be honest. No matter what you think, honesty is the best policy.

A young man came straight out of Special Operations training to my assault team. The stories of his performance during this long course had preceded him to the team. I knew I was getting a top performer and he would be welcomed with open arms. I counseled him on what I expected and he did not disappoint. Over the next several years, we both clawed our way further up the food chain to the point that I was his Troop Sergeant Major and he was one of my Team Leaders. By this time we had become very good friends. It reached the point where he signed his emails to me "From your little brother." He did this to be goofy but in all reality it was true. He had a lot of the same tendencies I had. He liked to train hard but, sometimes, he was in a little trouble for speaking a little too loudly at the wrong time; something that I may have had problems with during my Army career as well.

As a team leader, he did a great job. However, there were things he did that didn't sit well with his men and his leaders, me being one of them. I continued to be his biggest fan but I did not counsel him honestly as I knew I should have. It seems the close bond we had formed made me want to protect him from the negativity.

One day the Troop Commander came to me and laid it down. He said I needed to counsel him and counsel him hard and honestly. So, here I am getting counseled on my lack of honest counseling. This was a real eye opener. I sat down across the table from my soldier and I laid it out. I gave him the list of positives and then I laid out, more specifically, the negatives which had been hurting him and his team. He had

> been so busy while focused on training his team he may not have noticed his own shortcomings. When the counseling session was over, he shook my hand and walked out. It didn't take him more than a week to fix all of his personal and team deficiencies. So once again, I, as his leader, had failed. I had postponed the inevitable. He was a great soldier and just needed to be put back on azimuth. Luckily, I had an awesome troop commander who could counsel me on my poor counseling abilities. This is just another reason that leaders from the top to bottom can't be afraid to get in there and fix a situation if it is broken. This is for real.

In the above situation, I almost exacerbated the problem. But my leader stepped in with some hard counseling. I thought this was going to be a difficult situation but it wasn't. Once the truth came out and the deficiencies were noted, they were fixed immediately.

Tell your people what they need to know to fix the situation. They deserve it.

I point out this shortcoming of mine for the simple fact that I was able to mature as a leader through this learning experience. You must continue to learn and be open to criticism if you ever expect to become a "Great Leader."

Counseling behind your back = Gossip

How do you like it when people talk about you behind your back? Better yet, how do you like rumors and negative discussions about you occurring without you knowing? I am sure you wouldn't like it. Gossip is not counseling. So, if you don't like it, don't do it to your people. Speak to their face. Don't talk behind their backs. If you want your team to perform, don't be divisive with your people. You immediately lose your integrity and credibility when you're not up front with your people.

I remember a certain story about a manager at a large company who was hired to help turn a company in the right direction. He was doing what he could, but that wasn't good enough. I am not sure if he was counseled, but I doubt it. The man who was his leader would not tell him his performance was substandard and that he would be fired in a few days. One Friday, the manager went out and bought a house near where his new company was located. Everyone knew he was buying a house but his leader did not counsel him on his poor performance until after he made the commitment on the house. He lost his job the Monday following the purchase of the house. He ended up having to move to where he found a new job. Now he struggles to pay the mortgage on a house he has to rent out due to the crashed housing market. This is poor leadership. Letting this happen to someone, even though you plan to fire them, is unacceptable. You should still treat this man or woman with dignity and respect.

Honest counseling will be appreciated. You appreciate it, so why wouldn't the people who work for you appreciate it? Give it a try. It is great when you can speak the truth and get results. This will make your work environment much better for all involved. There won't be any questions as to how you feel about their work. Your people will have clear guidance on what type of performance is needed to be successful with you at the helm.

Thick skin is a prerequisite

Performers understand and are challenged by an area that needs improvement; they will be up to the task.

When I retired from the Army, my wife and I started a small business which dealt with tactical equipment and training. The training focused on small arms skills as well as the tactics to make military and law enforcement officers successful on the battlefield or in the street. After growing the business for a few years, we decided to expand the training side and hired a few men with whom I had worked with in the Army. These are A-type personalities, all of whom are hard chargers. Most of them worked out well. However, one in particular seemed to have a hard time working for someone who held less rank in the Army than he did, furthermore, he had an even harder time working for my wife.

Of all the people whom I have met in the business world, I must say that my wife uses less sugar coating than any of them. She says exactly what she feels so she can right the ship or fix the problem immediately. You will always know where you stand. No time for small talk. Get the problem fixed and move on. This didn't go over well with this one man in particular. He was offended when she would make corrections or speak up if his performance was less than optimal. She wanted him to perform at the high level of which she knew he was capable. This never worked out. His skin was extremely thin when counseled by a female and there was no rectifying the situation. Even 20 years in the Army may not prepare you for situations you will have to deal with as a civilian.

I think back about what could have been done differently with this scenario and there really isn't anything that could be changed. If you have strong leaders who are confident with what they say and do, you must have team members who understand that vision and don't get their feelings hurt when they hear the truth.

Below you will find a Special Forces Team Sergeant's Checklist, his reasoning behind the checklist, and the actual initial counseling statement which he provides to his soldiers upon their arrival to his team. This is very straight forward, but once again, a successful leader uses a checklist and is organized in order to take care of their people.

Basic Special Forces Initial Counseling Checklist

Operational Detachment- Alpha (ODA) Initial Counseling

    1) Background:
        a. Family Life
        b. Hobbies
        c. Education
        d. Previous Work Experience (Non-Military)
    2) Military Background (past NCOERs and ERB)
        a. Previous Units
        b. Deployments

[Non-Commissioned Officer Evaluation Report (NCOER): A report that is used to evaluate the NCO on their duty performance and their potential for duties with greater responsibility. The five key components of the NCOER are: competence, physical fitness and military bearing, leadership, training, responsibility and accountability.]

[Enlisted Record Brief (ERB): a single page summary of the service member's career to date, to include: awards and decorations, military and civilian education, deployments, duty assignments, amongst other things.]

3) Individual
    a. Near Term Goals
    b. Long Term Goals
    c. Overall outlook/impression of Special Forces
4) ODA TEAM
    a. Expectations on the Team
    b. Duties and Responsibilities (Rank/Job/Military Occupational Specialties (MOS) specific)
    c. Training Mentality/Focus of the Team
    d. Family Focus
5) Questions / Concerns

How the checklist is employed:

Here is what I use as a checklist for my initial counseling. I use it has a guide, a reminder to make sure I hit everything that I want to talk about when we sit down for the first time. Usually I will have it printed out, along with the Service Member's (SM's) initial counseling statement, his NCOERs and ERB and will put check marks by the items as we go through it, just to keep me on track.

My intent is to put the individual at ease at the beginning of the session and get him talking about himself as much as possible. That is why I start off about his background and family life. I will sit back and try not to inject too much besides questions regarding his background, where he grew up, what he did before the Army, how many kids, etc. My overall goal is to put him at ease and get them to talk about what they like to do… hobbies, etc. to see what they are truly passionate about.

Once we have exhausted that topic, the conversation typically transitions to Army experience. We will go through their ERB/NCOERs and talk deployments, previous units, and their overall experience with the Army to date. This is where we hit up past leaders, what has worked, what hasn't worked, etc. for the SM. From that point, we will move onto their Near Term and Long Term goals that they want to accomplish while in the Army. If the individual has been in Special Forces for a bit, I usually ask them what they think about Special Forces, and try to get a sense of their overall impression. This is a rabbit hole of a question, because the conversation can easily head off on a tangent, but it does a good job of giving me an idea of what this SM wants out of Special Forces. Maybe that's prepping him for the long walk or getting him another skill set that might open his eyes to the full spectrum missions and operations that we as a Regiment are involved in. Not until we are through all of that is when I start doing the talking. I will read him his initial counseling statement which outlines my philosophies, the team's focus, duties and responsibilities, etc. After reading the counseling statement, I talk a bit more about what I expect of my guys on the team during day-to-day activities, training and operations. I always end the counseling session with a chance for the individual to bring up anything that we didn't discuss that he feels I should know about from the beginning.

Usually I set aside about an hour for the initial counseling session. We do it in the Team Room at my desk, which is isolated from the rest of the guys. If the opportunity allows, I try to get the other guys out of the room so that it is quiet and the SM is put at ease and willing to talk about sensitive issues if need be.

Initial Counseling Statement:

Initial Counseling For:
SSG Joseph Dirte
ODA XXXX

This is your initial counseling. This counseling is intended to provide you with the necessary purpose and direction to carry out your responsibilities as a Junior 18 Bravo - Special Forces Weapons Sergeant on ODA XXXX

What I expect of you:

<u>TEAM FOCUS</u>

The focus of this team is and will be the conduct of combat operations. Our primary focus is Special Reconnaissance (SR), but it will not be our only focus. Given the ever-changing face of the enemy, we as a fighting element must be prepared to conduct Unconventional Warfare (UW) at a moment's notice. The current definition of UW is:

> **Activities conducted to enable a resistance movement or insurgency to coerce, disrupt, or overthrow a government or occupying power by operating through or with an underground, auxiliary, and guerilla force in a denied area.**

Memorize it. Know it. We must strive to always improve our Tactics, Techniques and Procedures (TTP) for all types of missions across the Special Operations spectrum. As an SR team we will build on the wealth of knowledge that the current team members' possess to increase our capabilities and more importantly our lethality.

CHAPTER 32 COUNSELING

Military Free Fall (MFF) Operations are an important part of ODA XXXX's capabilities; however it is still only one of many INFIL techniques. THIS IS NOT A SKYDIVING TEAM. When ODA XXXX conducts MFF Operations, it will be with the strict focus on the ability to conduct combat operations once the infiltration phase of the mission is complete. Once team members have attained LEVEL 1 Status, all jumps will be conducted with Combat Equipment.

Language. It is time to re-focus our energies on the basics of what made SF "special." We will be given the opportunity to study and master our target language... I expect each member of ODA XXXX to excel and strive for a minimum of 1+/1+ rating on the OPI or DLPT.

PHYSICAL CONDITIONING

Physical Conditioning is paramount in this business. Your physical condition directly affects the detachment's ability to execute its missions. Long dismounted infiltration and exfiltration with casualties is the standard. To ensure each individual can meet this standard we will conduct a Physical Readiness Test (PRT) and build endurance events into both PT and training. We will conduct Team PT 2 days a week with one of the days (usually Friday) consisting of a competitive team event.

The PRT will consist of the following 10 events: (1) 1 min pushups (2) 1 min sit ups (3) 1 mile run (4) weighted rope climb (5) max pull ups (6) max dips (7) 5 mile ruck march @ 45 (8) 2 min Tire Flip (9) shuttle run (10) combatives – 3 x 2min rounds (stand up, grappling, full MMA).

TEAM LIFE

We work in a dynamic environment and our training will reflect this fact. Training will be challenging, designed to push each team member beyond his comfort zone. You need to be able to think on the move, quickly decide and act. Hesitation is not an option here. If you are running training I expect you to prepare and apply yourself to the event to produce a professional product. Every training event should have a technique, physical and psychological component. I expect you to be proactive and speak up if you see a deficiency in our TTPs. Along with that, you should take ownership of skills you possess and teach them to others. Request training time to teach the skills which you believe we need to be successful. Be on time and have your gear prepared ahead of time.

Many of our tasks are high risk: shooting, breaching, jumping and combatives are not without substantial risk. Therefore each member of this detachment must do everything in their power to minimize this risk. That means you must learn the tasks at hand well enough to recognize and prevent common errors. Take responsibilities such as RSO and Jumpmaster seriously; it is a matter of life and death. It is through our constant awareness that we can continue to beat the odds and keep detachment members safe. Read and know the Regulations that govern our training... and adhere to them.

Here in SF we have an officer problem. The officers feel they have to step in when things are not being taken care of by the NCOs and rightfully so. That is a direct reflection of Senior NCOs not completing their duties in a satisfactory manner. We must work to combat this situation. Every time we fail at a task, especially the basics (i.e. accountability, maintenance, training) we invite the officers into our world and allow them to take over. I expect you to take seriously your responsibilities in these areas and as a team we will keep the officers in their lane. When you give an "up" on gear or personnel, you had better be certain. This has a direct impact on the command's trust in us, and therefore the operations with which we are tasked.

INDIVIDUAL DEVELOPMENT

I expect you to take charge of your career and pursue those opportunities afforded to you in this battalion. We have access to many schools and courses which are unavailable to the majority of the Army. You are expected to give your maximum effort when tasked with one of these courses. Not only are you responsible for successfully negotiating the training, but also for bringing it back to the detachment and passing it on to your peers and subordinates. I hope you will advance your education, both military and civilian, while you are on the detachment. I will give you maximum opportunity to do so. Senior NCOs on the detachment will be expected to take an active role in counseling their junior counterparts. Sooner than you think, you will be a Team Sergeant and expected to run a detachment. Start preparing now. Ask questions. Develop your own philosophy on training and team life. Write down things that work and don't work in your opinion.

FAMILY

Team time will only last so long, and when it ends (and yes it will end) your family will be there. Take care of them. Keep me informed of any personal issues. Keep your family informed. I know Family Readiness Group (FRG) activities are not very popular with the wives and I understand why. However, in SF, it is essential that wives know one another, who to contact with a problem, and what their resources are if something happens. We will have regular team parties and social outings to keep the families in regular contact with one another.

BOTTOM LINE
- Show up to work on time, ready to go
- Eight hours bottle to throttle, no exceptions
- Plans are open to discussion until a decision is made, then execute
- Remember the reputation of the team directly impacts what missions we are tasked with
- Keep officers out of our business
- Conduct yourself as an adult and a professional at all times
- Keep me informed
- Take care of your family
- Read your manuals (SME for the team)
- Don't work out, TRAIN
- Team Mottos:
    o Competition Breeds Success
    o Look for Work

WHAT YOU CAN EXPECT FROM ME

I am a very straightforward person. I am only concerned about our ability to conduct our wartime and standby missions, and the guys I work with. In my role I have to balance the desires of the individuals with the needs of the team. I cannot promise you I will get you everything you want, but I will do my best, and if I can't you will know why. I will give you every opportunity to excel. I will give you honest feedback, including strengths and areas to improve upon. I believe in time off, and will strive to give you the most family time possible. I will give you the chance to pursue your individual goals within SF and the Army through schooling, deployments, training and positions of increasing responsibility. I will handle any issues you bring to me in a confidential and timely manner. If I cannot help solve the issue, I will find someone that can.

ADDITIONAL RESPONSIBILITIES

- Responsible for all aspects of Range Operations. Planning, reserving, concept and conduct of CMMS Ranges.
- Maintenance and accountability of all weapon systems, mounts, Nods, etc.
- Responsible for all Team assigned Vehicles to include weekly Motor Stables (PMCS)
- Learn from Senior members on the detachment

Statement of Understanding: I, _____
fully understand the content of this counseling session and will comply with the best of my ability.

Signature: _____ Date: _____

Mr. Team Sergeant
MSG, USA
Detachment Operations Sergeant

###

Lessons Learned

- A leader is a coach, a mentor, and a teacher.
- Have an entry interview with each new team member when they arrive.
- When you counsel your people, give it to them straight and let them fix the problem.
- When you are counseled, take it to heart and fix the problem

CHAPTER 33
DISCIPLINE

The military talks about discipline often but what is the true context of this term? Discipline can merely be the fact you do what you are trained to do under pressure. Or is discipline punishing those who veer from the path of some list of rules? Or is being disciplined having the courage to do what is right?

Leader or Disciplinarian

Many so called "leaders" I have met feel they need to discipline their people to constantly send the message they are in charge. You will listen to what they say, you will abide by their rules, no questions asked. This is not a culture of discipline. This is a culture of tyranny. Anyone can threaten and punish those who work for them. It takes a dedicated and talented leader to establish a group of disciplined followers; disciplined in that they stay on course out of respect for their leader and for the mission at hand.

As Colonel Rounds said in northern Iraq, "Punish the deserving." This is true of those who work for you as well. There are people who will need to be disciplined for their actions and there are those who need very little watching because they are self-disciplined. You must determine who is who and not use group punishment. Group punishment has never, and will never, work. Respect those who follow the law and *punish the deserving*.

Don't confuse a culture of discipline with a tyrant who disciplines. The latter creates an organization which is dysfunctional. Many organizations will function with a disciplinarian at the helm. They will continue to produce as long as the disciplinarian remains aggressive and continues to micromanage and threaten their followers into performance (or submission). Once the disciplinarian leaves, the organization will crumble. With no one to herd the sheep, the flock will be lost. If you want to achieve greatness not just in the present, but create an organization whose greatness will continue long after you leave, you must establish a culture of discipline. An organization which is disciplined in their actions will be successful long after you have retired or moved on. What would make you more proud, the fact they couldn't survive without you or the fact you built an organization whose legacy is a testament to your leadership and discipline?

Blind-sided Discipline

Are you implementing regular counseling sessions to your people about their shortcomings or are you gossiping behind their back and telling their peers instead? Organizations which keep the truth from those who need it are doing a disservice to everyone involved. Ultimately, these actions can have detrimental effect on your organization's morale. Poor morale is a symptom of poor communication. Bad news doesn't get better with time. Take a minute to challenge those who are not performing to meet your expectations and see what happens. If they go to pieces, then you have a quick answer. However, you may be surprised when they step up to the plate and quickly overcome the challenge. No matter what the performance of anyone in your organization is they deserve to know what is expected and how they are performing.

Most individuals want to perform. Don't blind-side them. This is disrespectful and will not have positive results. No matter their performance, everyone deserves respect.

Stop Doing the Wrong Thing

Once you know the *right thing*, do you have the discipline to do the right thing? Equally as important, do you have the discipline to stop doing the wrong thing?

How do you stop doing the wrong things in leadership situations or curb poor performance on your part? I have found most successful people keep task lists or, as some say, a "to do" list. Many call this a punch list. So you have a list of tasks which must be performed to reach what you call success. Where do you keep the list of things which cause you to perform poorly?

Stop Doing List

I recommend a *Stop Doing List*. By self-evaluating you can write down the most critical stumbling blocks at the beginning of your task list with a "Stop Doing" in front of the short falls. An example would be those of you who like to micromanage. This is a common weakness especially for new leaders who have not gained confidence in their own skills as a leader, but also lack confidence in the skills of those they are leading. Take your list and put "Stop Micromanaging" right at the top of the list. You will quickly see that those words on your task list make the problem more easily identifiable. You will step up to brief your group and, as you do, the first note tells you to stop micromanaging. This might just make your meeting a little shorter which will make everyone a little happier.

As a Special Operations leader, I would be tasked with a mission. I was briefed as to my left and right limits and sent forth to do great things… or at least capture a lot of terrorists in the process. I was sent to a remote base far from the flagpole with a group of disciplined operators. Everyone knew the mission and everyone gave their all to help move towards mission completion. Discipline, as a leadership trait, is highly sought after and, in some organizations, hard to come by. We had very disciplined men in our organization who kept the distractions to a minimum. As a leader, this made life easy; focus on the mission at hand and ensure the soldiers had what they needed to complete their tasks. Once I left this organization, they never missed a beat. They were successful in spite of my absence. I consider this complete success.

Lessons Learned

- Don't confuse a culture of discipline with a tyrant who disciplines.
- Group punishment does not work.
- Inspire intense commitment from your people so they create a disciplined organization which will last long after you are gone.

LEADERSHIP TOOLBOX

CHAPTER 34
ARE YOU CONSCIOUSLY COMPETENT

Years ago while working in the technology department of a school district in North Carolina, my wife, Melynda, came home talking about a class she had participated in which addressed competence. As we discussed this class I became more intrigued by the discussion and wanted to analyze how I fit into this system with regard to the skill sets I was using in the military. We have since discussed this many times. I always analyze what I am doing and what I am teaching to ensure I am giving students what they need to be successful on the range or in a tactical environment.

First, we should note there is a little confusion as to who came up with this theory. Some say it was Confucius, while others say Socrates; yet some claim it was W. Lewis Robinson, who happened to be an industrial training executive. The bottom line is the origins of this theory are not known and really don't matter. What is important is how this theory relates to leaders and leadership.

So lets discuss the levels of competence or the lack thereof.

The Conscious Competence Theory [1,2] allows us to explain the levels of learning one goes through when developing a new skill or behavior. But what does this have to do with leadership?

I have always believed that a leader should be introspective. Part of understanding yourself is looking deep inside and being honest with what you find; honestly evaluating what you feel, how you act, and why you feel and act that particular way. There must be a reason for your actions and feelings and you need to understand it. The Conscious Competence Theory provides an excellent framework in which to analyze your leadership skills.

Unconsciously Incompetent

More than likely, this is where you started. You didn't have a clue and didn't have a clue that you didn't have a clue! Knowledge may be power but ignorance is bliss. Life is good when we don't know what we don't know. This unconsciously incompetent state conjures memories of life as a private at the beginning of my career in the Army…

> *"Hey Private Lamb, we need a box of Grid Squares, go get 'em from supply." Of course there isn't such a thing as a box of grid squares, they are the squares (grid lines) drawn on military maps. As a private I didn't know any better, so off us privates would go looking for grid squares, canopy lights (another item that didn't exist), or the keys to Area J. Area J was a wide open training area on Ft. Bragg that definitely didn't require a key. I was lucky enough not to get sent to the First Sergeant to get the Prick E-8. The unsuspecting Privates that fell for this hoax were rewarded by a Crazy Panamanian First Sergeant smoking them up and down the hallway with push-ups, pea pickers, you name it they did it, old school Cross Fit. For those of you that didn't get that prank, a Prick 77 is a radio, Prick is slang for AN/PRC. Most radio gear had the acronym AN/PRC that*

stood for Army/Navy, Portable Radio Configuration, thus the name Prick 77. Well a First Sergeant's grade is an E-8, so if one went to the First Sergeant asking for a Prick E-8, trouble no doubt would ensue. Of course I do believe the First Sergeant enjoyed this as much as those who sent the unsuspecting Privates off to the butcher.

The life of a private poses the perfect framework of someone existing within the unconsciously incompetent state, not knowing what they do not know. Life is simple. Life is good… until you are shown you are behind the power curve as a leader. Leading isn't easy and you will absolutely not be successful if you are *unconsciously incompetent*. As leaders, we must be aware that there are *unconsciously incompetent* people operating in and around our battle space. You may have subordinates who fit into this category. Part of being successful as a leader is reading people. *Unconsciously incompetent* individuals must be sorted out quickly. If this level of performance applies to someone's leadership skills then we don't want this person in a leadership position until they have progressed to a satisfactory level. However, just because someone is *unconsciously incompetent* in one area of their needed skill sets doesn't necessarily preclude them from being extremely competent in another equally important area.

Consciously Incompetent

This is where you need to be in order to start learning. You must be aware you don't know what is going on. You are *conscious* of the fact that you are *incompetent*; this is where learning begins. For those of you who don't have an issue with admitting you are not educated or have more to learn in a certain area, you are already headed towards success. For the rest of you, those who feel they already know everything; you need to grow a little. Every one of us can learn, unless you think you already know it all. Then I would not put you in this category. Instead, I would put you in the *unconsciously incompetent* category and that is where you are going to remain until you reach some level of self-awareness. As a leader, look around and find those who admit their shortcomings. They are teachable, trainable. Being teachable applies to you too. Even now, I try to learn something new in every class I teach. Every single class has something to offer me even though I am the instructor.

Consciously Competent

Now we are getting somewhere. Through practice we have attained a level of expertise which allows us to *consciously* move through the steps to be successful at a task. We have become aware of our new skills and are working on refining them through deliberate effort. Generally speaking, I feel this is where most of us operate. If, in addition to being *consciously competent*, you can successfully describe what you are doing in order to teach others to be consciously competent, you are above and beyond most in your field. As a leader, you should constantly try to understand why you are doing what you do. You should be able to outline the steps necessary to make sound leadership decisions on the battlefield or in the boardroom. When I decided to write this book, I thought I had battlefield leadership figured out. Now I would say I understood it well, but have continued to learn as I wrote this book and talked to trusted sources that are successful military, law enforcement, and business leaders. As a soldier turned businessman, I have a goal to become *unconsciously competent* in the art of leadership. However, while we do examine the steps of our new skill, we want to ensure we are always operating in the real world and not in an academic world. Slipping into an overly analytical mindset won't work when you need to make sound leadership decisions quickly. "Paralysis through analysis" is what some call this. I have no use for academic theories which are not applicable in the real world.

Unconsciously Competent

Now we are getting into the PhD side of learning. Through practice, repetition and real world experience, we have attained a level of expertise that allows us to *unconsciously* move through the steps to be successful at a task. The skill we are learning has become second nature or instinctual. We perform the skill much quicker and smoother because it does not require conscious thought. We have become so adept at our new skill that we may be able to do it simultaneously with other actions. However, don't get too wrapped around the axle if you are doing a great job and can't completely explain the steps you followed to get there. You are still a success. I see a lot of this in the shooting courses I teach. A huge percentage of tactical shooters who are very good at what they do cannot teach it. They aren't able to analyze their performance to the extent which would allow them to teach others. It takes a tremendous amount of discipline for someone to remove themselves from their *unconsciously competent* mindset and dissect what they are doing in order to explain it to others. If you are able to *unconsciously* complete the leadership task at hand and teach your subordinates how to do the same, or at least elevate them to the *consciously competent* level, you are doing great things.

Leadership Complete Competence

Now that you have an idea of your level of competence, can you teach leadership? Teaching is a whole lot more difficult than just filling a position. If you are teaching a drill which requires coordination, such as throwing a ball or shooting a pistol, the results are easily quantifiable. You do this step and then that step and it will lead you to the desired result. Leadership training is not nearly as cut and dry as other skill sets. You cannot simply follow a flow chart and end up at *great leader*. With all of this being said, you should continually try to mentor your up and coming leaders. Your long-term goal is to build an organization which is much stronger than any of the individual leaders in it. Your departure should not cause concern with anyone. You have put a strong leadership network in place which will thrive without you.

If you are the teacher, you must have a grasp on the levels of competence and understand how to progress from one level to the next. Some of your "students" will not make it to higher levels. Therefore, they will not get promoted. You must make honest assessments of these individuals. If you advance a man or woman into a leadership position that is *unconsciously incompetent*, you may destroy your organization. Morale will suffer with *incompetent* leaders in charge. However, if a leader is in the *consciously incompetent* category, we have something with which to work. This individual has made a step in the right direction by acknowledging they don't know or posses a certain skill. Admitting a shortcoming is a huge step in one's development.

**Tools for teaching your subordinates –
The Briefback**

Before any commander sent his men on a Special Operations mission, they were required to conduct a Briefback. A Briefback was attended by all of the individuals involved in the operation and was directed to the leaders at the lowest level. The reason for the Briefback was not for the commander to micromanage what was going on. This brief was

CHAPTER 34 ARE YOU CONSCIOUSLY COMPETENT

targeted at the individuals who would be on the ground (or in the air) and anyone else who was in a direct or supporting role of the mission. What I realize now is this allowed everyone to fully understand not only what was expected of them, but what their secondary responsibilities were as well. In order for the team to be successful, all of the individuals involved needed to understand what their responsibilities were and, beyond this, they needed to understand the responsibilities of their leaders. This is important because key leaders were sometimes taken out of play. This was mostly due to communication issues but there were rare occasions when aircraft had maintenance issues or vehicles didn't make it to the target area. Maintenance is a nightmare in a desert environment. What if the key leaders were wounded? After the Briefback, we all knew what the commander's intent was for this particular mission. In addition to knowing the step by step of the mission plan, the Briefback allowed all those involved to speak up if they realized something wouldn't work on the ground as briefed. This particular commander's tool was almost as important as a rehearsal. Normally, when chasing a time sensitive target, you didn't have time for a full blown rehearsal. The Briefback was as good as it was going to get. This is the most important part of the planning process. You get the needed information out to all who will be involved. Not only will subordinates know what is expected of them, they will be more efficient on the battlefield because they understand the entire mission. They are not required to lose their momentum by awaiting further guidance from their chain of command. They know what needs to be done which allows them the ability to seize the initiative. Those who don't care for this process remain mired in the slow, methodical procedure called the Military Decision Making Process (MDMP). MDMP is too slow to catch innovative enemies, too restrictive for self-starters (such as Special Operations soldiers) and doesn't get every member of the task force involved in the planning and Briefback of the mission. In the end, the Briefback is pushing your subordinates to become at least Consciously Competent, if not Unconsciously Competent, at the task at hand. They understand the mission and the steps needed to achieve mission success.

Competence

At the end of the day, you need competent leaders no matter what your mission happens to be. It is a good idea for you, as a leader or as a follower, to know where you fit in the competence equation. However, just second-guessing your leader is not being competent. Anyone can sharp shoot a leader. Instead, put yourself in his or her shoes and devise a better solution. Why do you think they fell short? What is available to make you more competent? What training will take you to the next level? When you are selected for a leadership position, what will you use as your checklist so you avoid the same shortcomings?

Truly competent leaders will have the confidence to pick the most *consciously competent* or, better yet, *unconsciously competent* subordinates to help them reach mission success.

Lessons Learned

- Constantly work to develop all of your skills, including leadership, through the four levels of competency.
- Use the Briefback format with your team. Everyone must understand the entire mission.

CHAPTER 35
KNOWLEDGE DOMINANCE

You have all heard the old adage "Knowledge is power." But is this true? If you are in charge and you hoard all the knowledge, you will indeed be powerful in your own pathetic little world. However, in the grander scheme of things, you will be very limited in what you can accomplish if you, as a leader, keep all the cards to yourself. In order to be efficient and successful, we need as many people as possible involved in the knowledge process. There are benefits in having more than one brain in the game.

When the Global War on Terror (GWOT) first picked up steam after 9/11, we thought we were making progress in the world of hunting terrorists. We did, in fact, grab a good basket full of low hanging fruit around the world. But after each mission, we hit a dead end. Terrorists arrested, questioned, and then, more than likely, released after a few months. Of course, with as large a net as we cast, we were bound to get a few big name terrorists. It is just the law of averages. The problem was we had a system for catching them but not one for retaining them. We often joked about the catch and release system in place. In fact, I think there were some patches floating around with "Terrorist Catch and Release Program" embroidered on them. This is "funny" until you are on your third or fourth tour in Iraq hitting the same house and arresting the same individual time after time. Of course, after a while these terrorist suspects knew the system better than we did.

So what was the problem? Well, we had some info, but not the whole picture. Sometimes we had enough info to find these guys. But did we have enough to hold them? As an organization, the U.S. military is very good at its job but it has limitations. Some of these limitations are real and some are very real. In other words, there are limitations which impact the military's effectiveness in accomplishing their mission of capturing or killing terrorists.

What is the problem?

There are many long arms of the law which feel they can nab wanted terrorists by themselves. The problem is there are very few organizations that have the ability to be the action arm of the law *and* do the dirty work of detaining the terrorists afterwards. The military has the system in place to detain but they may not always have the system in place to figure out who should be detained. Or, once detained, how the detainee can lead us to bigger fish.

So, after a couple years of this system not working satisfactorily, we had to wake up. We had to get *everyone* at the table to contribute so we could hunt these men to the ends of the earth together.

As I said, the military's system was great for a group of operators to go out, bonk someone on the head, and bring them back to be thrown in jail. But what about after that? The system just wasn't working. We needed all of our organizations and individuals, regardless of title, to work together.

Hoarding Information

Some individuals look at the phrase "knowledge is power" as a blue print for personal advancement through the hoarding of information. Each new piece of data they gather is jealously guarded and used for their own agenda. These individuals will eventually find themselves separated from the group. Whether your work place has a business mission statement, commander's intent, or just plain goals, knowledge/information must be spread to everyone all the time so the whole organization can succeed. Withholding information to make yourself feel powerful is unacceptable and, in the end, a path to mission failure.

To improve this system, we needed everyone at the table telling everyone else at the table what they knew and what needed to be done. In order to be more successful, the man on the ground needed to be able to talk directly to the intelligence officer who knew the personality we were tracking. The operator needed to be able to talk to the interrogator about what he saw when the suspect was arrested. We needed everyone to know what everyone else was thinking and what they were doing. We needed knowledge dominance.

What is Knowledge Dominance?

Everyone must be on the same sheet of music. We must share absolutely everything we know with everyone present and work together constantly. This will allow us to use every strength of every individual for the greater good of the group and the mission. For those who like the power of knowledge, or should I say the power of keeping that knowledge from their people, you will not like this system. In the system of which I speak, you will be a member of a team. All participants are giving all they have to accomplish the mission. Every organization is dedicating their assets to the mission. They are not holding back assets simply because they may not get the glory. The glory is to accomplish the mission and win.

What are your goals?

One of the issues we ran into was who would take credit for the operation. Luckily, we had military people who didn't really want any credit. They just wanted to get out there and find the bad guys. Their reward was capturing or killing this person. Those who felt they needed to take credit could if they wished. Of course, working with someone who always wants the credit is hard; they are not in it for the right reasons. But, if having someone take credit allows the military to get their guy, the credit problem can be handled. Don't get me wrong, there were many great organizations pulling their fair share to accomplish the mission and not asking for any credit. These are the organizations which continue to be incredibly successful and are the go-to organizations when we need help.

What it isn't.

Knowledge dominance is not forwarding every email you get to all of those folks who work for you. It is your job to extrapolate the needed information or meaning from that email and put it in a concise version to pass on. If you are the email forward king, you have already lost everyone's interest. If it is important to tell your people why, do it up front.

I cannot stress enough the importance of knowledge dominance. After seeing what operations using knowledge dominance achieved, and the percentage of terrorists who remain detained, I was a believer. I could tell by the progress we were making on the High Value Target (HVT) list that things had radically improved. We were steadily taking the terrorists off the street so they couldn't harm any more innocents or develop any more networks.

Call it what you want. It doesn't have to be *knowledge dominance*. The key is that every person involved with the process, whether it is hunting men or selling clothes, must know what all the other members are capable of and how their capabilities can be used to get you to your goal or finish the mission at hand.

If you are in business, the same is true. You must be able to work effectively by passing on information. The more brains dedicated to the problem, the better. You may not know who you are dealing with in your own business. You may have experts right under the tip of your nose who will step up and be the key to your overall success.

Lessons Learned

- Everyone at the table needs to know what everyone else at the table knows.
- Knowledge IS power and it must be shared with the members of your team to be efficient and successful in accomplishing the overall mission.

CHAPTER 36
WISH LIST OR CHECKLISTS?

When I became a young paratrooper in the 504th Parachute Infantry Regiment, 82nd Airborne Division, I watched with amazement as young Jumpmaster Sergeants stood in front of hundreds of troopers and presented the pre-jump briefing. We stood in sawdust pits looking up at the briefer and giving the correct reaction when he hit certain parts of the briefing. When the Jumpmaster said, "hit it," we all snapped into a good tight body position as though we had just exited a high performance aircraft while sounding off with, "one thousand, two thousand, three thousand, four thousand." We all kept our chins on our chest as though we were waiting for the opening shock of our parachute. As the Jumpmaster continued with the brief, we simulated each of the emergency procedures which he described. It is important to know exactly what you should do if there are problems during your jump. If you have twisted risers, they are quickly cured by a bicycling motion with your legs. If you have a partial deployment of your main parachute, you deploy your reserve parachute. But you deploy the reserve parachute in a specific way by throwing it down and in the direction of the spin.

This briefing was a show. The Jumpmaster had countless hours of rehearsal in order to stand in front of his peers, speak loudly and with extreme motivation and confidence, while not missing a beat and never referring to his notes. This show convinced every paratrooper that the Jumpmaster was all over it. As a young trooper, I was truly impressed. All the Jumpmasters in the 82nd were respected by the lower ranking soldiers.

The pre-jump briefing is required before every jump which you make or attempt to make. Sometimes Mother Nature just won't cooperate. So, I had literally stood and watched these pre-jump briefings close to one hundred times. After leaving the 82nd, I moved onto Special Forces. In Special Forces, soldiers aren't so excitable. When it is time for a pre-jump it is normally read from a book. I was a little embarrassed to see a Jumpmaster stand in front of the formation and read the briefing word for word. What was this all about? In the 82nd Airborne Division he would be laughed off the stage. I leaned over and made a smart comment to one of the guys beside me and all he said was, "Hey Lamb, this ain't the 82nd, relax bro." Relax??? This guy is the Jumpmaster and he needs to use notes?!?!? I was not impressed.

It took awhile for me to understand there were reasons the 82nd Jumpmasters put on the show they did. First, it was impressive and built confidence with the young soldiers who largely make up the only airborne division in the free world. Second, they are the 82nd Airborne. This is what they are known for. They are The Airborne.

In Special Forces, jumping out of a perfectly good airplane is just one task of many which fall under their specialty. One day you may be static line jumping using a round parachute which deploys by being pulled from its container by a static line attached to the aircraft. The next day you may be conducting a High Altitude Low Opening (HALO) jump or Military Free Fall (MFF) jump as it is called. In the civilian world this is called skydiving. After this you may be firing a machine gun, doing medical training, or practicing a foreign language. Oh, and don't forget, you have to make a little time to eat snakes…

The point is your Mission Essential Task List (METL) is significantly longer as a Special Forces soldier than as a paratrooper. You don't have the time to practice a Jumpmaster briefing for static line one day and then be expected to accomplish the same for a HALO jump mission the next.

Here is where checklists come into play. They work at the extremes. Specifically, a checklist is important for those who are new to the game or for tasks you are required to perform only now and again. Additionally, there are the tasks you find mundane because they happen every day. These also require a checklist to ensure you don't skip steps because you are comfortable with the tasks at hand.

Take a look at pilots. Every time a pilot gets into an aircraft they use a checklist. They follow this checklist in order to ensure they don't overlook a mundane task which could lead to a missed safety check which, in turn, could lead to a crash. A good rule of thumb is this: If the pilot isn't using a checklist, get out now.

So, exactly how does a checklist apply to leadership? Isn't leadership that feeling in your gut as you step into the spotlight in front of a hushed crowd and inspire a bunch of followers to get in line for the greater good? Absolutely not and a checklist is not a laundry list of how you want to act or feel. A checklist is a step-by-step guide to get you through a specific process. An example would be the *Team Leader Brief* for a Special Operations soldier conducting any type of mission, not just a direct action mission.

Direct Action: Short-duration strikes and other small-scale offensive actions conducted as a special operation in hostile, denied, or diplomatically sensitive environments and which employ specialized military capabilities to seize, destroy, capture, exploit, recover, or damage designated targets. Also called DA.[1]

__Team Leader Brief__
Introduction (Team Composition)
Primary and Alternate Tasks
Routes and Order of Movement
LCC Procedures (Last Covered and Concealed Position)
Primary and Alternate Breach Points
Primary and Alternate Internal Responsibilities
Coordination Points (Limits of Advance, Sniper Observer Positions, leader locations)
Post Assault Procedures and Responsibilities
Exfil Plan and Order of Movement
Contingencies
Special Weapons and Equipment
Any other information pertinent to all

This checklist isn't intended to be memorized. It is intended to be used. Every team leader would use this checklist. If he didn't have one, another team leader would hand him one to use as a reference as he briefed. In some briefing areas Army leaders have went so far as to blow this reference up and hang it on the wall for all to use while briefing. More often than not you can judge the efficiency and experience of the men in your midst by what is on the walls of the briefing area. Focused leaders will have needed references available for all; this will lead to efficiency and reliability during hasty planning sessions for Time Sensitive Targets.

CHAPTER 36 WISH LIST OR CHECKLISTS?

Why would you need to follow a simple checklist without memorizing it? In a perfect world with a rehearsed briefing, this list would not be required. However, we won't be working in a perfect world when we need to use this checklist the most. We will be operating in a strange environment while lacking sleep and good food. And most likely, we will be a little anxious if we are heading out the door to conduct a real world mission in some Third World city. We must always prepare for the worst. During our training period we must force ourselves to build checks and balances into the planning process so that during times of stress or exhaustion we will have reliable techniques that are tested and proven. Checklists fit perfectly into this category. In a crisis, we must not skip steps in the briefing process because lives depend on it.

Civilian leaders already benefit from using checklists. They have processes which must be followed. These are simply checklists. Quality assurance checks to ensure your product meets consumer needs. A checklist to ensure equipment is shipped in a timely manner and the correct product arrives at the proper location. Don't become complacent. Your customers have other choices they can make if you aren't meeting their needs.

> *We used checklists to ensure the proper equipment was loaded and weighed in a timely manner when we were deployed for missions around the world. We had a strict timeline the leaders had to follow. Once the alert was given, everyone had to be at the Fort in an extremely short amount of time. Once there, we had to ensure all our gear was loaded onto the correct vehicles. We used a color code, team designation tag system that made this possible, every soldier knew the system and could easily distinguish who the kit belonged to. This system also works well in the civilian*

> *world to ensure accountability. Normally civilians are not as concerned with property accountability as military operators. If your business is worried about the bottom line, accountability is a great place to start if you want to raise your profit and stop making redundant purchases.*
>
> *Once loaded, we had a brief amount of time to get all the vehicles weighed, the loads balanced and drive to a nearby airfield. Once there, we immediately loaded everything onto awaiting aircraft and strapped down the vehicles and containers. Leaders then conducted a manifest call to ensure all personnel were present and all gear was accounted for. We were loaded and on our way in less time than it takes most people to get up, eat breakfast, and drive to work.*

Other examples of using checklists which are extremely near and dear to my heart are calls for fire support and medical evacuation (MEDEVAC). When we needed bombs or helicopter gunships to engage enemy targets which could not be easily engaged from the ground, we used a specific *call for fire* sequence to get the needed help. Basic calls for fire when dealing with Army helicopters were relatively easy. However, when dealing with Air Force or Navy aircraft, a call for fire checklist, called a 9 line, was used to give the pilot the required information in a quick, concise manner. When attempting to get a MEDEVAC bird to land to save life or limb, we were also required to use a specific checklist. Everyone in the force understood exactly what the procedure was and had a checklist to get the pilots the much-needed information in order to get them on target as soon as possible. This is truly a matter of life and death. Obviously time is of the essence when calling for fire or evacuating wounded soldiers.

CHAPTER 36 WISH LIST OR CHECKLISTS?

Tom Davin, CEO of 5.11, a Duke University "Magna Cum Laude" graduate, a former Marine Corps Infantry Captain, and also happens to have an MBA "with distinction" from Harvard Business School, had this to say when I questioned him on his use of checklists.

"As the CEO of 5.11 Tactical, a fast growing product company, I receive confusing communications on a daily basis. Frequently, I have to ask a business partner or colleague "what is the problem you are attempting to solve?" or "would you provide some additional context before you recommend a course of action?" While I've trained myself to respond in this Socratic manner, I'm generally thinking "how about some SMEAC?"

Situation – Mission – Execution – Admin/Logistics – Command/Control = SMEAC.

"SMEAC is a military acronym used to summarize the five paragraphs of a basic operations order, a mental checklist. I was introduced to SMEAC during Marine Officer Candidate School at Brown Field in Quantico, VA. Often dripping with sweat in the sweltering July heat as my hand put pencil to paper, SMEAC brought order to the chaos around me as it became part of my wiring. It does the same today as every problem or opportunity gets run through this tool as a key element of my planning and communication protocols.

Often busy executives (or busy people) want to jump right to Action or the Execution part of the plan. At best, this runs the risk of others not fully understanding

your plan and choosing not to follow you. Doing the internal work of SMEAC may involve 30 seconds of mental analysis and visualization for a simple, time sensitive situation or it may require several days of strategy work for a major presentation. SMEAC provides leaders with both the planning tool and the delivery framework. By reviewing the context and mission or problem to be solved prior to outlining the actions or Execution, the leader establishes the "why" behind the proposed actions. Execution outlines the key "what"/"how" elements. Admin/Logistics and Command/Control are the supporting elements that complete the plan.

SMEAC also provides the framework for subordinate leaders to communicate to their teams, ensuring consistency of the message and a higher likelihood of vigorous implementation. So, whether you are planning a family picnic or the turnaround of a major corporation, start with SMEAC and act with the confidence that you are leveraging a tool proven by decades of United States military experience." (T. Davin, personal communication, April 2, 2013).

Being successful in either business or military callings requires checklists. As you can see with Mr. Davin's quote above, he continually falls back on the time tested Marine Corps training which he received many years ago.

Tom Davin has taken 5.11 to the next level through the use of his military leadership techniques. 5.11 is the hands down leader in tactical apparel for Law Enforcement professionals. He has expanded 5.11's reach into the outdoor and hunting market as well. Significant growth every year speaks volumes about a company and its leaders.

You should always have a plan. If you head into the boardroom, or onto the battlefield, you should be prepared to react to the changing situations around you. A checklist will prepare you for this situation. Most importantly, it will provide you with contingency planning options. A checklist isn't just about combat missions. It is about performing your leadership duties efficiently.

With experience comes comfort. With comfort comes complacency. And with complacency comes failure. Checklists keep you from becoming comfortable, becoming complacent, and becoming a failure.

The most elite counter terrorist soldiers in the world use checklists. Why wouldn't you?

Lessons Learned

- Use checklists for tasks at both ends of the spectrum. Critical tasks, mundane tasks, and tasks you perform infrequently.
- Situation – Mission – Execution – Admin/Logistics – Command/Control = SMEAC. Tom Davin, CEO 5.11

CHAPTER 37
COLONEL JOHN BOYD AND THE OODA LOOP

These days it seems leadership books aren't complete without a chapter, or at least a few token paragraphs, about Colonel John Boyd. So here is my chapter. However, I have a different approach with regard to Colonel Boyd.

Just to get everyone on the same track, Colonel Boyd started his career as a member of the Army Air Corps. He later transitioned into the Air Force as a fighter pilot. He would go on to develop a number of theories which would change military thinking. Many consider him one of the greatest American military thinkers of the 20th Century.

Colonel Boyd was instrumental in changing the way pilots and aircraft engineers thought about aircraft. Boyd developed the Energy-Maneuverability (E-M) Theory. This theory described the performance characteristics of a given aircraft through both mathematical equations and graphs. For the first time, an aircraft's capabilities could be predicted and described in order to be studied in a scientific manner. Colonel Boyd's theory revolutionized air to air combat. Now, with the appropriate data, an aircraft's strengths and weaknesses could be determined ahead of time and, as a result, a pilot could determine the ideal way to fight his plane against an enemy's. Colonel Boyd expanded his theory and used it to help design the next generation of American fighter aircraft. This theory has little to do with leadership but it is one of the cornerstones of modern dogfighting.[1]

One of Colonel Boyd's other well-known theories is the OODA Loop. Several business and military leadership courses consider the OODA Loop the Epic Leadership Theory. The OODA Loop is designed to put you ahead of your enemy in not only your thought process, but in your final decision and action process as well. There are literally hundreds of books and professional papers which examine and analyze Boyd's OODA Loop but I am going to summarize it here and show how it applies to leadership.

The OODA Loop stands for:

O-Observe
O-Orient
D-Decide
A-Act

Using Colonel Boyd's own words, here is his bullet point description of the OODA Loop levels:

Observe - Unfolding circumstances, outside information, unfolding interaction with the environment, and implicit guidance and control.

Orient - Cultural traditions, genetic heritage, new information, analysis and synthesis, and previous experiences.

Decide - Decision.

Act - Action[2]

This all seems a little confusing at first, but in reality this is what we do every day without thinking through the situation. What Boyd did was break down our mental process into distinct stages and analyze each one. Given a situation which would be influenced positively by very timely decision making (like a dogfight), Boyd provided a model with which to quickly work through the decision making process. The OODA Loop's goal is to help someone make a decision, the correct decision, faster than their opponent. This is a good thing.

So how does this influence leadership? Frequently, I have heard presenters discuss the OODA loop and describe how it ends with the correct decision which leads to overall mission or business success. This is where we want to be but let's slow down a little and analyze what really put us in the correct decision making process.

At the heart of Colonel Boyd's OODA Loop was training. He didn't miraculously start using the OODA Loop one day. He trained for years and years to hone his quick decision making process. Known as "40 Second Boyd," he had a standing challenge to any other fighter pilot that he could beat them in aerial combat in 40 seconds or less. He even allowed the opposition to start in a position of advantage before the fight ensued. In spite of starting at a disadvantage, Colonel John Boyd never lost this challenge. He did this due to years of training, experience, and fighting efficiently through the OODA Loop process. He didn't just train. He trained using complex, realistic scenarios which would allow him to sharpen his skills to a razor like edge. Sometimes we only train to the lowest standards. Colonel Boyd never did this.³

Take another look at the OODA Loop process.

Observe - You can observe all you want but are you seeing what really needs to be seen? Are you looking at the right things? In order to focus on problem solving, we must know from where problems originate. This ability comes from training. By training I do not mean one day with a leadership expert but from many experiences, which ingrain the correct observation focus into your daily pattern of observation. A simple way to think about this is through the question: Are you seeing the trees or the forest? In leadership, great leaders see both. Leaders need to be able to step back and see the big picture, i.e. the forest, but still possess the ability to drill down and identify the key components which may need our specific attention, i.e. the trees.

Orient - All other inputs aside, previous experiences are key. I understand your heritage as well as your traditions will have an impact on your orientation, but it is past experiences gained from training and possibly past failures which will help build your base of knowledge.

Decide - Your decision making process relies heavily on past training experiences or past real life experiences... period. Cut past the fluff to what really matters.

Act - An action you take in training can be right or wrong, but, either way, you will learn from that action. As a result, you will be much more likely to make the correct decision the next time around. I have learned more from mistakes during training than perfect experiences in real life.

In other words, training for a task ahead of time allows us to move through the OODA Loop faster when that task needs to be done for real.

Another often overlooked fact about the OODA Loop is Colonel Boyd intended for this process to be used at the lowest levels of decision making. This tool isn't reserved for Generals and CEO's (although they are allowed to use it).

CHAPTER 37 COLONEL JOHN BOYD AND THE OODA LOOP

It is for you and me, the front line leaders or, better yet, the decision makers on the ground. Those closest to the action are the ones in the best position to observe, orient, decide, and act. As a leader, you have to ensure your people have the knowledge and training to take maximum advantage of the OODA Loop from their frontline position.

The OODA loop applies to Leadership. This is undeniable. However, as leaders we need to empower our people to move efficiently through the process unhindered by our micromanagement and heavy handedness. If you want to be successful, you must be surrounded by people who can make decisions and it is up to you, as a leader, to train them to do so.

To better understand your subordinates' requirements you should work through different possible crisis situations which may affect your business, unit, or community. For example, in Law Enforcement the simplest task can turn into a full blown catastrophe if we don't act quickly. Prior to the day of crisis, your people must work through the possible scenarios. As they move through the "what if's," your people must understand they are ultimately responsible for making the important decisions on the ground. This doesn't come naturally to some, so you may need to work through numerous scenarios to get the desired decision making processes ingrained into your subordinates. Even more important, we need to push our subordinates to make decisions, work on their process, and force them to get involved. This will allow all members of your team to make needed decisions quickly to avert a possible disaster.

After many scenarios and plenty of training, your people will be able to use the OODA Loop to quickly arrive at the correct decision.

Here are the areas we want to focus on and improve upon during OODA Loop like training:

Rapid Information Processing - in the beginning, information processing will be slow and methodical since it may be a new way to look at events as they unfold. However, by building your experience level, you will eventually be able to *rapidly process information.*

Rapid Option Analysis - once you have processed the information, you will need to analyze your options. In the beginning, this will be a slow and tedious process which may involve asking others for their opinions. Once you have worked through decision making processes in numerous training or real world scenarios, you will quickly speed up your option analysis. Eventually the *rapid option analysis* will come with your increased experiences.

Correct Decision Making - *Correct Decision Making* is the goal, but this won't initially be the norm for inexperienced men and women new to the quickly developing situations around them. Some may make quick decisions, but they may be wrong. If this happens, you have just learned something. After several scenarios and many incorrect decisions, you will start to figure out what really should have been done. If you are making correct decisions easily, take the training to the next level by adding more complexity and try to involve other business colleagues, support personnel, or fellow officers.

So does the OODA Loop apply to leadership? Undeniably.

The OODA Loop definitely applies to Leadership, but the key piece is to build you and your people's experience level over time with training and real life experience. This will be the key to successfully negotiating the OODA Loop.

CHAPTER 37 COLONEL JOHN BOYD AND THE OODA LOOP

This chapter barely scratches the surface of Colonel John Boyd's body of work. To find out more, read one of the hundreds of books or articles about his theories.

Lessons Learned

- A leader improves his OODA Loop skills through constant training and real life experience.
- Not only does a leader need to develop their own OODA Loop skills, he must develop his subordinates' as well, especially if they are the decision makers in the organization.

"The only man who never makes a mistake is the man who never does anything."

-- Theodore Roosevelt

LEADERS ON THE HOMEFRONT

CHAPTER 38
FAMILY LEADERS

As a leader, it can be hard to look past your responsibilities and day to day grind to see other leaders who are making an impact on your life and other lives around you. If you take the time and look, you'll find the most awe inspiring acts of leadership happen right under your nose.

Leaders, whether they are CEO's in the business world, members of law enforcement, or military personnel, often look within their own profession to find other leaders to emulate. However, if you stop and think for a moment, you may find the most respected and truly reliable leaders in your life are closer than you believe.

How about your spouse? I know you are the big, tough, barrel chested freedom fighter, but who works with you the most to ensure your success? More than likely, it's your husband or wife.

In my case, it has always been my wife. She has helped steer me in the right direction or, if on the rare occasion I decided to provide the Commander's Intent, took charge and led our family to mission accomplishment.

Of all the leaders, who is more important in making decisions in the absence of any guidance than the ladies who raise our children and support the home front?

When you are down and out, who helps clean you up and get you back in the fight? Who has seen you at your best and worst? For me that answer is truly my wife. I am extremely grateful for all she has done and continues to do for me every day.

> *In the case of my wife, she was forced to carry the heavy burden of burying my mates when their bodies were returned home. This is a task that no one takes lightly. Other members of our task force faced not only the burial process, but the notification of next of kin, a task in which you only get one chance. I have been very fortunate that I have never had to notify any next of kin. I have seen the toll this takes on soldiers who are forced to pass on the worst news a spouse could receive. Worse yet, having to tell a Mom or Dad their child has made the ultimate sacrifice. After the notification, my wife was a part of the grieving process, from helping with children to organizing food for the families. But the most trying part is always the funeral itself. She watches the weight of the world come crashing down on these family members' shoulders as they come to grips with the final realization that their loved one will not return from war.*

> *When my wife faced this daunting task, I was still deployed. There were a couple occasions when friends were killed and I was in the United States. But, for the most part, my wife had the responsibility of burying the soldiers with whom I served. This is an unbelievable burden. She, and all of the other wives, had to step up to lead their families and fellow spouses in order to, as my great leader Jon H had said, "do what needed to be done." This mantra applies not*

only to you on the front lines, but to all of the leaders supporting our cause.

On the home front

How did I do as a family leader? As they say, hindsight is 20/20. As I look back to the great career I had in the Special Operations community, I am proud of my accomplishments. However, on the home front, I would say I could have done better. My wife's only requirement from me was that I take care of her. I am not sure I did a perfect job there, but I must say, we are a pretty good team.

Now that I have separated from the military, I have realized what is really important in the long run. Family. If only we could apply the same great leadership principles from our day job to our family life we could "kill two birds with one stone". Or, as my more peaceful friend Amarett would say, "feed two birds with one handful of grain". You need to realize this now, while you are still serving. This realization will only make your team stronger. Whether you are in the military, law enforcement, or own your own business, you will be better off if you have a great leadership life at home with your family.

I worked in the highest levels of the Special Operations community. Our main priority was the military mission, which makes sense. It wasn't stated out right, and no one really wanted to admit it, but families came second. The mission was always the highest priority for these top shelf units. There was a belief that in order to get the job done, you had to give all of your devotion to your performance at work. However, when it was all said and done and you finally walked away, you are no longer a member of the team. This is not something I say with negativity, this is reality. I am not in any way a part of the team with which I served with for 15 plus years. I am now, more than ever, reliant on my family and true friends for support. This is a lesson I had to experience to learn. I hope you can make the move towards taking better care of and leading those who truly care about you sooner than I did.

What does it take to be a leader in your family?

Your tasks as a family leader are pretty easy to define: pay the bills, yard work, and keep your home in good working order. However, what about the other areas for which you are responsible as a family leader?

Being your family's Emotional Leader is a key role. Being stable as you deal with your family is even more important than being an emotional leader at your job. Very often this is not the case. Leaders can be all over this responsibility at work but when they arrive at their home, they shut down. They fail to use the same leadership skills with their families which they preach all day with their team. At least that is how it was for me. I wanted to relax and reflect when I should have been more aggressive in leading my family. The Army received the best performance I had as a leader while my performance at home left a lot to be desired.

Give your spouse and children the same cheerleading you give your co-workers. Motivate your kids so they perform to impress you as the family leader. My children are unbelievable achievers. Their mom was always there to do whatever they needed to support their mission. She still is. My kids understood I would be absent for many key events because of my commitment to my military unit but that still did not make it acceptable.

CHAPTER 38 FAMILY LEADERS

You should be the spiritual leader for your family. This is a mission we must not fail. How you train your children in their spiritual life is a legacy which has a much higher priority than the legacy you leave at your day job. When you are long gone, your children will be carrying on as you trained them. Will you be proud of their performance?

Set examples for your kids to follow. They look to you as role models and will emulate your behavior. Additionally, you must be a bold and decisive leader for your family but also one who is willing to show compassion and caring when needed. Stand up for what is right and do not be afraid to be a man. Our country needs men serving their families.

Great leadership for our country starts at home. If our country starts to stumble, it is because of poor leadership at home. Poor leadership will destroy us in the long run. Do you want a strong America? If so, know that a strong America starts at home. Many of you working in the military, law enforcement, or the business world are there to serve your country. Never forget how much being a great leader for your family serves your country as well. Of all the organizations in America, the ones she needs most to succeed are her families.

Take a minute and look at your situation. If you don't have a good leader working with you as your spouse, then you are truly missing out. More than likely your spouse and children are there and you need only pay attention to see family leaders who will be there for you when you most need them. More importantly, they will be there long after you have hung up your spurs and moved out to pasture. Your family should be the most important legacy you have as a leader. Be proud of your family and see they are in this to win, just as you are.

Lessons Learned

- Earlier in this book I asked you to think about who the leaders were in your life. After reading this chapter, would your answers change?
- Do you want a strong America? It starts at home.

ACKNOWLEDGMENTS

Leadership in the Shadows is a miracle. First, you have a farm boy from South Dakota (me) who didn't impress his English teacher, Mr. John Kinder, very much with his grasp of the written English language. But yet, here is my 3rd book Mr. Kinder.

How would I ever survive as a Private in the 82nd Airborne Division? SGT Jack F stepped up and became a great leader to follow and a mentor to constantly emulate. He motivated me not only with his professionalism but with the push-ups he made me perform when he saw I needed more mentoring. He and I have become great friends over the years. I owe SGT F.

As a completely green Special Forces soldier, I met SFC Ray C while I was with 5th Special Forces Group. SFC C set the example for speaking his mind and getting things done. He could always back up his banter and continues to be a great friend. I can never repay him for the wall-to-wall counseling sessions he has given me over the years. To this day, he is the only man who gets away with calling me "Boy."

After leaving 5th Group, I moved to an Army Special Mission Unit (SMU) where I was placed in the charge of SGM Jon H. He wasn't a SGM then, but it didn't take him long. I watched as Jon H performed his leadership duties and led from the front at all times. He took it personally when it came to training his team and his troop. He had the right *combat mindset*. Jon continued to occupy leadership positions above me throughout my time in this SMU. This was a true blessing. His leadership formed me into what I am today.

When I stumbled, he punished me but he never gave up on my future as a leader.

I only served under CW3 Mike H for a year, but we have since become great friends. He was a long time 1st Special Forces soldier turned Warrant Officer. He would fall into the category of "Mr. Sunshine" to those of you who know him but, even with his grumpiness, he would continue with the mission when others would stop to rest. Mike has always been completely honest with me and every other person with whom he comes into contact. I have tried to be like him when I can. Not the grumpy part, just the straight shooter trait.

These are just a few of the men who I have looked up to as a military man. I can guarantee that life would never have been as great as it has been without a few others who have stopped to help me along the way. The first is my Father. My Dad was a great man. He was a man of few words but was a hard working cowboy farmer who meant what he said. After my Dad passed away, another old family friend, John Cone, stepped up to help me continue what my Dad started. He is always ready to teach or listen depending on what I need.

I had almost thrown in the towel on **Leadership in the Shadows** when an email came in from Matt Bucella chastising me for the delinquent delivery of this book. At that time I decided if Matt really wanted to see it finished, I would enlist his help. Not sure how a Navy Flyboy turned Ft. Lauderdale cop became involved in this process but I could not have done it without his honest feedback and incredible insight. He pushed me when I hit the wall and I am grateful.

Once again the citizen soldier, Master Sergeant Kevin Dorsh, has come to the rescue. As he fought for our country deployed overseas as a Special Forces' Team Sergeant, he also worked during his off hours to edit this book. His insight is what was needed to truly give you, the reader, what you wanted. It has been a pleasure for me to see Kevin grow as a leader in the US Army. From the first time I shot with him in the tunnels of Panzer Kaserne, I knew he would go onto do great things for our country. He has not disappointed.

To Eric Poole, former Marine, Virginia Military Institute Graduate, and *Intermedia Outdoors' Guns and Ammo Magazine* editor, thanks for the additional help with this project. I am sure we have many more subjects to cover in the future.

To the Warriors across this country who have helped educate me to be a better instructor, thanks. Many of you had to sit down and explain exactly how your organizations work and what the "process" was. I have learned so much and plan to continue this learning and growing process. From law enforcement to unfamiliar branches of the military to the business world, we are forever in your debt for your service and patience as you deal with the varying degrees of leaders and the politics that affect your day-to-day service.

This book has been sent to my former place of employment for the redacting process. I have done my best to keep the stories readable but sterile. I appreciate the effort the intel community has put into keeping me straight. But then again, they are used to following me around and picking up the pieces when I break things.

Lastly, to my wife Melynda, thank you. This process would have been much simpler if she would have written this book. Her insight is incredible. I have learned so much from her by watching her as a wife, mother, teacher, mentor, and now, CEO. She doesn't mess around, doesn't pull punches, and isn't afraid to get her own hands dirty on a daily basis.

APPENDIX A

Congressman Murtha

Please show this to President Clinton and Sec Aspin. I request that you not make it a public document.

Operation on 3/4 Oct '93 in MOG.

I. The Authority, Responsibility and Accountability for the Op rests here in MOG with the TF Ranger Commander, not in Washington.

II. Excellent Intelligence was available on the Target.

III. Forces were experienced in Area as a result of six previous operations.

IV. Enemy situation was well known
- Proximity to Bakara Market (SNA strong point)
- Previous reaction times of bad guys

V. Planning for Op was bottom up not top down. Assaulters were confident it was a doable operation. Approval of plan was retained by TF Ranger Commander.

VI. Techniques, tactics and procedures were appropriate for mission/target.

VII. Reaction forces were planned for contingencies
 A. CSAR on immediate standby. (UH60 with medics and security)
 B. Ranger Co (G) as ground reaction force in armored Humvees
 C. 10th Mtd Div QRF (coordinated with / not organic)

VIII. Loss of 1st Helo was supportable. Pilot penned in wreckage presented problem.

IX. 2d Helo crash required response from the 10th MTN QRF. The area of the crash was such that the SNA were there nearly immediately so we were unsuccessful in reaching the crash site in time.

X. Rangers on 1st crash site were not penned down. They could have fought their way out. Our creed would not allow us to leave the body of the pilot penned in the wreckage.

XI. Armor reaction force would have helped but casualty figures may or may not have been different. The type of men in this task force simply would not be denied in their mission of getting to their fallen comrades.

XII. The mission was a success. Targeted individuals were captured and extracted from the target.

XIII. For this particular target, President Clinton and Sec Aspin need to be taken off of the blame line.

William F Garrison
William F Garrison
MG
Commanding

NOTES

Chapter 12 - Moral Fiber

1. Child, Michael S., Sr. *Memorandum for the Inspector General, Department of the Army, Subject: Review of Army Inspector General Agency Report of Investigation (Case 10-024).* (Virginia: Department of Defense Inspector General, April 2011), pp. 1-6.
2. Coram, R. Boyd: *The Fighter Pilot Who Changed the Art of War.* New York, NY: Back Bay Books. 2002. Print, p. 281.

Chapter 13 - A Leader's Courage

1. Hastings, Max. *Inferno.* New York: Vintage Books. 2012. Print, p. 325.

Chapter 18 - Earning Mentality

1. Giduck, John. *Terror at Beslan: A Russian Tragedy with Lessons for America's Schools.* Colorado: Archangel Group Inc. 2005. Print, p. 28.

Chapter 19 - Credibility

1. Garrison, William F. Letter to Congressman Murtha, "Operation on 3/4 Oct '93 in MOG." *Philadelphia Online* | Blackhawk Down N.p., N.d., Web. 04 August 2013. <http://inquirer.philly.com/packages/somalia/dec14/garrison.asp>

Chapter 26 - Avoiding Bureaucracy

1. Bureaucracy [Def. 3]. (n.d.). In Merriam Webster Online, Retrieved August 12, 2013, from http://www.merriam-webster.com/dictionary/ bureaucracy.
2. Lockstep [Def. 2]. (n.d.). In Merriam Webster Online, Retrieved August 12, 2013, from http://www.merriam-webster.com/dictionary/lockstep.

Chapter 31 - Compliance vs. Commitment

1. Buell, T. *The Warrior Generals: Combat Leadership in the Civil War.* New York, NY: Crown Publishers, Inc. 1997. pp. 218-234.

Chapter 34 - Are you Consciously Competent?

1. MindTools.com. "The Conscious Competence Ladder." *MindTools | Learning Skill | The Conscious Competence Ladder* N.p., N.d., Web. 12 August 2013. <http://www.mindtools.com/pages/article/newISS_96.htm >
2. businessballs.com. "Conscious Competence Learning Model." *businessballs | leadership/management | Conscious Competence Learning Model* N.p., N.d., Web. 12 August 2013. <http://www.businessballs.com/consciouscompetencelearningmodel.htm>

Chapter 36 - Wish List or Checklists?

1. Joint Chiefs of Staff (US). *Department of Defense Dictionary of Military and Associated Terms* (Joint Publication 1-02). Washington, DC: US Department of Defense. p. 81.

Chapter 37 - Colonel John Boyd and the OODA Loop

1. Coram, R. Boyd: *The Fighter Pilot Who Changed the Art of War.* New York, NY: Back Bay Books. 2002. Print, pp. 135-153.
2. Ibid, pp. 327-344.
3. Ibid, pp. 101-120.

REFERENCES

Bowden, M. (1997, December 14). Black Hawk Down: An American War Story. *Philadelphia Inquirer.* Retrieved from http://inquirer.philly.com/packages/somalia/dec14/garrison.asp

Buell, T. (1997). *The Warrior Generals: Combat Leadership in the Civil War.* New York, NY: Crown Publishers, Inc.

businessballs.com. (2013). *Conscious Competence Learning Model.* Retrieved from: http://www.businessballs.com/consciouscompetencelearningmodel.htm.

Coram, R. (2002). Boyd: *The Fighter Pilot Who Changed the Art of War.* New York, NY: Back Bay Books.

Department of Defense Inspector General. (2011). Memorandum for the Inspector General, Department of the Army, Subject: Review of Army Inspector General Agency Report of Investigation (Case 10-024). Arlington, VA: Michael S. Child, Sr.

Giduck, J. (2005). *Terror at Beslan: A Russian Tragedy with Lessons for America's Schools.* Bailey, Colorado: Archangel Group Inc.

Hastings, M. (2011). *Inferno: The World at War, 1939-1945.* New York, NY: Alfred A. Knopf.

Joint Chiefs of Staff (US). (2013). *Department of Defense Dictionary of Military and Associated Terms (Joint Publication 1-02).* Washington, DC: US Department of Defense.

MindTools.com. (2013). *The Conscious Competence Ladder.* Retrieved from: http://www.mindtools.com/pages/article/newISS_96.htm.

ABOUT THE AUTHOR

SGM (R) Kyle E. Lamb served in the United States Army for 21 years. The vast majority of that time was spent in leadership positions in the Special Operations Community. Throughout his successful military career, SGM (R) Kyle Lamb filled key leadership positions across the operational continuum with Special Operations Units during wartime operations. Some of these positions of elevated responsibility included Assault Team Leader, Sniper Team Leader, Troop Sergeant Major, Combat Development Sergeant Major, and Task Force Sergeant Major.

Kyle Lamb is a recognized industry leader in innovative tactical marksmanship shooting techniques as well as the key designer of several combat proven tactical products. He has contributed significantly to federal and local law enforcement agencies as well as the Department of Defense by providing unequaled tactical instruction and leadership training.

Kyle Lamb founded Viking Tactics (VTAC) in 2002 and has served as its president ever since. Kyle has developed VTAC into a credible and respected company in the tactical community. Viking Tactics leadership, tactics, and firearms instruction are highly sought after commodities. VTAC has been able to provide real world experience to military and law enforcement students. Additionally, Lamb has been asked to assist several large private sector businesses with leadership evaluation and development. This priceless experience has helped develop VTAC's outstanding reputation.

SGM (R) Kyle E. Lamb is also the author of ***Green Eyes and Black Rifles: Warriors Guide to the Combat Carbine*** and ***Stay in the Fight!! Warriors Guide to the Combat Pistol***. Lamb has produced several Carbine and Pistol Instruction DVD's that are available from Viking Tactics, Inc.